# Photojournalism Disrupted

*Photojournalism Disrupted* addresses the unprecedented disruptions in photojournalism over the last decade, with a particular focus on the Australian news media context.

Using a mixed-methods approach, the book assesses the situation facing press photographers and their employers in the supply of professional imagery for news storytelling. Detailed qualitative case studies looking at special events and crisis reporting complement a longitudinal study of sourcing practices around everyday events. Additionally, interviews with industry professionals offer insights into how news organizations are managing significant structural change. Ultimately, the book argues that photojournalism is being reshaped in line with wider industrial disruptions that have led to the emergence of a highly casualized workforce.

As a comprehensive study of contemporary photojournalism practices, *Photojournalism Disrupted* is ideal for scholars and students internationally, as well as (photo)journalists and media professionals.

**Helen Caple** is an Australian Research Council Discovery Early Career Researcher Award Fellow and Senior Lecturer in Journalism at the University of New South Wales, Australia. Her research interests centre on news photography, text-image relations, and discursive news values analysis. She is currently exploring the role of citizen photography in contemporary journalism. Helen has published in the area of photojournalism and social semiotics, including *Photojournalism: A Social Semiotic Approach* (2013). She is also the co-author (with Monika Bednarek) of two books examining the news media: *News Discourse* (2012) and *The Discourse of News Values* (2017).

# Photojournalism Disrupted
The View from Australia

**Helen Caple**

Routledge
Taylor & Francis Group

LONDON AND NEW YORK

First published 2019 by Routledge

2 Park Square, Milton Park, Abingdon, Oxon OX14 4RN

605 Third Avenue, New York, NY 10017

*Routledge is an imprint of the Taylor & Francis Group,
an informa business*

First issued in paperback 2022

Publisher's Note

The publisher has gone to great lengths to ensure the quality of this
reprint but points out that some imperfections in the original copies
may be apparent.

*British Library Cataloguing-in-Publication Data*
A catalogue record for this book is available from the British Library

*Library of Congress Cataloging-in-Publication Data*
A catalog record for this book has been requested

ISBN: 978-1-138-31677-5 (hbk)
ISBN: 978-1-03-233833-0 (pbk)
DOI: 10.4324/9780429455469

Typeset in Times New Roman
by Apex CoVantage, LLC

# Contents

**6 Professionals and amateurs: are we all in this together?** 87
*Australian photojournalism disrupted 87*
*You are now entering the precariat: proceed with
    caution 94*

# Figures

# Tables

# Acknowledgements

The ideas and words presented in this book were formed on the lands of the Bedegal and Gadigal peoples of the Eora nation. I would like to thank the traditional owners for their ongoing custodianship of these lands and recognize their continuing connection to land, waters, and culture. I pay my respects to their elders past, present, and emerging.

I would like to thank Bob Franklin for inviting me to participate in this series. Thanks also to the editorial staff at Routledge for seeing this book through to publication. Many thanks to the news editors who gave generously of their time and insights through interviews for this book. They are Neil Bennett (News Corp Australia), Carl Earl (Guardian Australia), Mags King (Fairfax Media), Phil McLean (AAP), and Stuart Watt (ABC News) – I am immensely grateful for your support of this research. And to my partner, Monika Bednarek, who continues to act as my sounding board and exacting proofreader, thank you for your valuable feedback, encouragement, and support.

This research was fully supported by the Australian Government through the Australian Research Council's Discovery Early Career Researcher Award funding scheme (project DE160100120). The views expressed herein are those of the author and are not necessarily those of the Australian Government or Australian Research Council.

# 1   Introduction

## A decade of disruption

There is not a single press photographer, photo editor, or photojournalism scholar who would dispute the fact that a well-crafted photograph makes you feel something, and it has long been stated that while people may forget what you say and do, they never forget how you make them feel.[1] These are dangerous words to begin a book about photojournalism with, but these are dangerous times for photojournalism. Photographs matter. We live in a world dominated by photographs. Almost every media text we engage with involves photographs. Digital storytelling is said to live or die by the photographs that accompany it, and digital storytelling is the coin that all news outlets now predominantly deal in.

In such an environment, one would expect professional photojournalists to be in constantly high demand. A few still are, but astoundingly, some news organizations are abandoning their photographers and replacing them with mobile phones, either in the hands of their wordsmiths (e.g. *Chicago Sun-Times*, see Channick, 2013; Anderson & Young, 2016, p. 298) or in the hands of the public (Anderson, 2013). Even more astounding is the thought that a stock photograph can do the work of a news photograph, yet this is being suggested by some well-respected journalism schools, with Poynter being a recent, if embarrassing, example (Hare & LaForme, 2018). After all, the photograph is just window dressing, an afterthought, a gap filler, right?

Wrong.

Press photographs are valuable content. Like the words that accompany them, press photographs are capable of carrying the full burden of news reporting (Caple, 2013). They need to be accurate, truthful, and accountable. Photographs need to be precise and specific so that they may educate

---

1 The original quote, "They may forget what you said, but they will never forget how you made them feel," is attributed to Carl W. Buehner.

and resonate. Just as well-crafted words will draw a reader into a story, an equally well-crafted photograph will encourage the reader to linger. To paraphrase one Australian photojournalist: Beauty, in a news photograph, not only makes you look, it makes you look for longer (David Maurice Smith at the Walkley Media Talks, Sydney, 2016). To this, I would add that when you look for longer, you begin to feel something.

As this book will document, photojournalism professionals and researchers are all in agreement regarding the importance of the news photograph. The question is, then, how have we arrived at the current situation, where both the photograph and the professional who makes it are being stripped of their hard-won value? Answering this question is the task of this book. It traces the disruptions that have precipitated the demise of the professional photojournalist, and importantly, it uses empirical evidence to assess whether the situation is as dire as these opening paragraphs suggest. Special focus is given to the Australian context, a very restricted market in terms of legacy news providers (Dwyer, 2016), which has been hit particularly hard by these disruptions.

Before embarking on this endeavour, however, a few points of clarification about the terminology used in this book:

*Photojournalism* refers to the act of photography production by professional photographers on behalf of a news organization and for publication as news reporting. I concur with Greenwood and Thomas's (2015, p. 629) assertion that "an image should only be understood as photojournalism if it aligns with the roles and responsibilities one would traditionally ascribe to journalists in a democracy". A *photojournalist, press/news photographer* would be the person tasked with producing photographs for publication in journalistic contexts.[2]

*Press/news/editorial photograph* refers to the single still photograph produced by press photographers for publication as news reporting.[3] Throughout the book, I use these terms interchangeably, along with *photograph* or *frame*. In so doing, I am referring to the photography produced by photojournalists that is usually published at news websites and in newsprint in the reporting of unfolding news events.

I use the terms *image/imagery/visuals* to refer to photographs (including generic/stock imagery) and other forms of visual representations (e.g. from screen captures or from video footage) produced by citizens and those who

2  When quoting or paraphrasing the research of others, I will maintain the terms used by them – e.g. Thomson (2018) uses the term "visual journalist". For a broader definition of photojournalism, see Campbell (2013, p. 11).
3  This excludes photographs that are also published in news contexts but are associated with opinion writing or sponsored content or advertising.

do not fall under the remit of journalistic endeavour, but which may at some point be published by the news media.

The book series in which this volume appears uses the term *disruptions* to signify the radical transformations in the journalism industry that have been precipitated by the intersection of digital technologies with the social, cultural, and financial conditions that are able to take advantage of them. The scale and pace of these transformations *disrupt* "settled understandings and traditional ways of creating value, interacting and communicating both socially and professionally and [. . .] trigger changes in the business models, professional practice, roles, ethics, products and even the accepted definitions and understandings of journalism" (Franklin, 2018). Campbell (2013, p. 7) further notes that disruption "is a product of more than competition alone, and occurs when technology transforms the economy". For the news media industry, the transformative effect of these disruptions has been exacerbated because "the arrival of the internet did not herald a new entrant in the news ecosystem. It heralded a new ecosystem, full stop" (Anderson et al., 2014, p. 83). This new ecosystem is one dominated by the digital screen, and it affects all aspects of news storytelling. It is an ecosystem that many news organizations sought to incorporate into traditional business models, rather than create separate, new business models that respond directly to this disruptive threat (Allworth, cited in Benton, 2012). As is well-known by now, the consequences for the legacy news media have been devastating.

In the remainder of this chapter, I document the disruptions that have led to the current highly precarious position of photojournalists and the ongoing undermining of their craft.

## A decade (or more) of disruption for photojournalism

Professional journalism in the twenty-first century has been marked by unprecedented disruptions in the form of institutional, technological, and social change. By and large, the industry response to such change has been to decimate staffing levels (Young, 2010; Skok, 2012; Zion, 2013) in the service of economic rationalism. Around the world, it has been the photography departments at news organizations that have been particularly savaged. In some cases, entire photography departments have been dismissed (e.g. *Chicago Sun-Times*, US), or depleted to skeletal levels (e.g. *Sydney Morning Herald*, Australia). In fact, the tenured staff position of the press photographer has been all but eradicated (Anderson, 2013; Allan, 2015; Thomson, 2018). There is not a single example of a news organization dismissing all of its *writers* and requiring its photographers to now provide both words and images. Yet writers are routinely called upon to capture images to go with their words, most often using a mobile phone (see Chapter 5). The implications of such disruptions are not to be underestimated, both in terms of the status afforded professional photographers and the photographs that they produce, and in terms of the values associated with the images that are likely to be used in their place. In the following paragraphs, I detail global trends in relation to the institutional, social, and technological disruptions of recent decades before honing in on the Australian context and the effects that these disruptions have had on this particular market. While these are disruptions that have affected the journalism industry more broadly, the purview of this volume is to focus on these disruptions in the context of photojournalism.

## Disruptions of a global scale

The US, UK, and Australian news media industries are experiencing the most serious contraction in their histories (Zion, 2013; O'Donnell et al., 2016; Pope, 2018; Thomson, 2018; Young & Carson, 2018). In the US, for example, newspaper employment has fallen by more than 50 per cent (Greenslade, 2016; Pope, 2018), while in the UK, the net loss of local newspaper titles stood at 228 between 2005 and 2017 (Kakar, 2018). In Australia, more than 3,000 editorial jobs have been lost in the last decade (MEAA, 2018, p. 4). Many news organizations continue to struggle to find sustainable business models that can replace the "rivers of gold" (Macnamara, 2012; Simons, 2012; Skok, 2012) that once financed the production of editorial content.[4] As a result, many media companies now run on skeletal staffing levels wherein the *multiskilled news worker* may be required to take on any or all such tasks as researching and gathering information, interviewing,

---

4  In the US context, print newspaper advertising revenue fell from about $60 billion to about $20 billion, between 2000 and 2015 (Thompson, 2016). And while one newspaper, *The New York Times*, was announcing a fall of 19 per cent in print ad revenue, Facebook, on the same day, was announcing a 59 per cent rise in its digital advertising revenue (Thompson, 2016). A similar picture emerges in the Australian context where newspaper advertising revenue has dropped 40 per cent in five years (Feik, 2017, p. 26). In Australia, the online advertising market was estimated to be worth $6 billion in 2017. However, the lion's share of this ($4 to $5 billion) would be generated by Facebook and Google (Feik, 2017, p. 26). According to figures cited in the issues paper [released on 26 February 2018 by the Australian Competition & Consumer Commission and seeking feedback on issues relevant to its Digital Platforms Inquiry], from 2011 to 2015, Australian newspaper and magazine publishers lost $1.5 billion and $349 million, respectively, in physical print advertising revenue, but only gained $54 million and $44 million in digital advertising (Taylor, 2018). On a global level, the two tech companies, Facebook and Google, are said to be picking up 80–90 per cent of all new digital advertising (Feik, 2017, p. 26).

and capturing images and sounds, to editing/producing, packaging, and publishing stories for print, web, and mobile devices. At the same time, the provision of content (both visual and verbal) is increasingly outsourced to news agencies (Gynnild, 2017; Láb & Štefaniková, 2017, p. 18). In relation specifically to photojournalism, a similar picture emerges. In the US, the job market for "visual journalists" was more than halved between 1999 and 2015 (Thomson, 2018, p. 803). As Thomson (2018, p. 803) notes, the ratio of reporters to photographers at *The Wall Street Journal* in 2015 was 2,000 to 1. Equally devastating is the fact that memberships in professional associations (e.g. National Press Photographers Association [NPPA] in the US) have more than halved over the last 30 years (Thomson, 2018, p. 804). Membership numbers provided by NPPA, as of April 2018, stand at 5,200. Fifteen years ago, this number was approximately 10,000 (NPPA, 2018, personal communication). Similar reports have emerged from the UK, where both local and national newspapers have laid off almost all of their photographers (Greenslade, 2012), with expense being cited as a key motivation. Putting it bluntly, Donald R. Winslow (former editor of NPPA's *News Photographer* magazine and website) states, "There are no patrons supporting photojournalism now. The patrons were newspapers and magazines. And they've cut off the money. That's just the raw truth of it" (cited in Estrin, 2017). This point is not lost on the professional photographers either, as quoted in the *State of News Photography* report commissioned by World Press Photo in 2016: "The first act of violence against a photographer starts with the lack of financial and contractual protection by the company that is 'hiring' them" (unidentified photographer, cited in Hadland et al., 2016, p. 24).

The loss of financial support for photojournalism coincides with the burgeoning of *free* content accessible online. Some news organizations even blame the large-scale layoffs of photographers on the ubiquity of *free* imagery online (Lang, 2011, referring to CNN's decision to lay off 50 photojournalists, technicians, and librarians). For a long time, researchers have noted the fact that citizens who witness major crises are now likely to not only film and photograph these experiences but also upload their imagery to social media platforms, where it can be readily accessed (often without cost) by news media organizations (Allan, 2013, 2015; Andén-Papadopoulos & Pantti, 2013, p. 960; Allan & Peters, 2015). In the context of breaking news, this new source of imagery poses a number of challenges to the news media industry. It has been widely acknowledged that citizens have little sense of journalism as they capture and share their personal experiences of what is happening around them (Pantti & Bakker, 2009; Allan, 2013; Becker, 2013). Rather, these images are "spontaneous, spur-of-the-moment responses, so often motivated by a desire to connect with others" (Taubert, 2012; Allan, 2013, p. 1). Neither are citizens governed by the same standards of ethics or credibility as professional journalism (Pantti & Bakker, 2009, p. 472). Thus, the imagery that they produce may be seen as a "non-conventional" or even "outlaw" view.

Such imagery may also bring with it different artistic and technical qualities, and a level of graphic/violent content (in victim imagery) not traditionally part of the repertoire of the professional photographer, who would usually be much later on the scene of a disaster and subjected to the usual restrictions imposed by the emergency services. Consequently, the rise in the sourcing of citizen imagery from social media outlets by the mainstream media has been matched by the rise in ethical, moral, and legal concerns (Zelizer, 1998, 2004; Sontag, 2003; Pantti & Bakker, 2009; Hoskins & O'Loughlin, 2010; Singer, 2011; Chouliaraki & Blaagaard, 2013). Given the concerns surrounding the use of citizen imagery at the time of disasters, news organizations that do publish such imagery routinely replace this with professionally produced photographs as soon as they become available (although the interviews conducted for this research study suggest otherwise – see Chapter 5). Likewise, the necessary and time-consuming process of verifying citizen imagery is also cited by interviewees in this book as a reason for not publishing such imagery (see Chapter 5).

Possibly the biggest threat to the tenured position of the professional photographer, however, is the practice of sourcing images from citizens for use in the everyday, routine reporting carried out by news organizations. This not only suggests that anyone can make photographs without the need for professional training or the need to operate within the professional ethical/ moral guidelines that guide all other aspects of news reporting. It further reinforces the suggestion that there is little to no financial value associated with the capture of photographs, since citizens are usually elated to have their images published and to see their bylines in print, and rarely accept payment for their use (István Virágvölgyi, former head of photo desk, MTI Hungarian News Agency, 2013, personal communication; Mags King, Managing Photo Editor, Fairfax Media, 2018, personal communication). However, the capture of a photograph has worth, no matter who is behind the lens, and as such should be financially remunerated. Citizens freely offering up their images for publication jeopardize the employment opportunities for photographers, as does the sourcing of images from social media without attribution, acknowledgement, or permission. Again, quoting from the *State of News Photography* report commissioned by World Press Photo in 2016, one photographer notes,

> I wish the newspapers thought of photography as an integral and important part of their publication, however I realize that they may just steal photos from social networks and publish them without paying.
>
> (cited in Hadland et al., 2016, p. 24)

The extent to which such practices are common in the Australian news media context is a key point that this book seeks to investigate. The empirical studies in Chapters 3 and 4 deal specifically with the issues of image-sourcing and attribution. The discussion so far also implies that historically, the press photographer has always struggled to attain full recognition for the art of visual news storytelling, and this point is taken up in the following paragraphs.

### *The value of the press photograph/er*

Several factors have contributed to the fraught history of the press photograph/er. Ambivalence towards the photograph itself has impacted on how press photographers have been treated throughout the history of the news media (Caple, 2010; Anderson & Young, 2016). Early historical accounts note the concern among Australian broadsheets of their newspapers being "downgraded by the photograph" (Evans, 2001). Similar concerns were expressed by American editors in the 1930s, who stated that photographs were nothing more than "a mechanical side-line to the serious business of fact narration – a social inferior" (*Time* editors, 1936, p. 20, cited in Zelizer, 2005, p. 174). Job security was also slow to come for the press photographer. It was not until the 1920s that the Australian broadsheets began offering full-time positions for press photographers, although Anderson and Young (2016, p. 4) note that the *Herald and Weekly Times* (a Melbourne-based tabloid newspaper company) employed its first full-time photographer in 1899. Attribution has also been slow to come to the photographer. As Chapter 2 will explain in more detail, it was not until the 1970s that photographers began seeing their bylines appear with the photography they produced for the news media (Reich & Klein-Avraham, 2014).

Historically entrenched attitudes such as these towards the photograph/er, along with the digitization of image capture and the explosion of *free*ly available images online, all seem to suggest that the decline of the tenured position of the professional photojournalist was an inevitable outcome of the disruptions of the last decade. As the final section of this chapter demonstrates, the result for the Australian news media context has been the decimation of the staff-employed/salaried photojournalist.

### The effects of disruptions in journalism on the Australian context

In 2018, the Media, Entertainment, and Arts Alliance (MEAA – an Australian trade union and professional organization, which covers the media, entertainment, sports, and arts industries) put the total number of Australian journalist/photographer job losses at more than 3,000 over the last ten years (MEAA, 2018, p. 4).[5] In addition to this high number of editorial job losses, another reason for focusing on the Australian context in this book is because Australia is a very restricted market in terms of legacy news providers (Dwyer, 2016), with Fairfax Media and News Corp Australia owning over 90 per cent of all newspapers between them.[6] This means that when journalists and photographers are made redundant, there are few alternative employers that they can turn to (cf. Fuller, 2014 on the rise in non-legacy/ traditional journalism jobs in Australia). The Australian Research Council/ media industry funded project New Beats has been investigating what happens to Australian journalists after redundancy. Their surveys reveal that on average, only 10 per cent of those made redundant still work in full-time journalism roles, with many working in multiple jobs, not always directly associated with journalism (Zion et al., 2018b).[7]

An important point noted by New Beats (2017, p. 3) in their submission to the Senate Select Committee on the future of public interest journalism in Australia is the fact that it is very difficult to gauge the exact number of job losses specifically among journalists and photographers. This is in part because some companies do not release information about job cuts, or provide only minimal details. In other cases, news of job losses does not distinguish between editorial and back-office staff (New Beats, 2017, p. 3). This means that much of the reporting and commentary on job losses are, therefore, best estimates, as are the figures reported on in this book. The focus also remains on those news organizations that are participating in the research project reported on in this volume – namely, ABC News, Fairfax Media, News Corp Australia, and Australian Associated Press (AAP).

---

5  To give some context to this figure, the 2018 *Newspaper Publishing Australia Market Research Report*, published in June 2018, put the total number of newspaper publishing employees at 13,907 (IBIS World, 2018). In 2010–2011, IBIS World reported that Australian newspapers had 23,472 employees (cited in MEAA, 2018, p. 4). The New Beats Project in Australia documents this contraction in the Australian news media context through a timeline visualization that documents reporting on all layoffs and publication closures since 2012. The visualization can be viewed here: www.newbeatsblog.com/ redundancy-timeline/.

6  Since completing the empirical studies reported on in this research, Fairfax Media has been taken over by Nine Entertainment (in December 2018), ending the historic newspaper brand after 177 years (Meade, 2018b). The merger resulted in the loss of 144 jobs spread across both organizations (Meade, 2018b).

7  Their research also investigated the effects of redundancy on professional identity values (O'Donnell et al., 2016; Sherwood & O'Donnell, 2018), and the full results of their research project (Zion et al., 2018a) can be downloaded from the New Beats website: www. newbeatsblog.com/.

Over the last decade, the two major Australian newspaper companies, Fairfax Media and News Corp Australia, have laid off thousands of newspaper staff, including photographers. In 2012, Fairfax Media shed 1,900 jobs, News Corp Australia (then News Limited) more than a thousand (Meade, 2014), with 45 of 270 News Corp photographers losing their jobs in that round of redundancies (Lee, 2012). Press photographers bore the brunt of the 2014 cuts, when Fairfax Media decimated its photography department (Bowers, 2014), shedding 75 per cent of its photographers and turning to Getty Images, among other agencies, to source its photography. This arrangement with Getty has now ended (see Chapter 5). In its heyday in the 1970s, the *Sydney Morning Herald*, one of Fairfax Media's flagship newspapers, employed 32 graded photographers and 6 cadets: In 2014, there were only 5 photographers left in Sydney (Anderson & Young, 2016, p. 295). In 2017, Fairfax Media journalists took strike action over plans to cut a further 125 editorial jobs. Just as these job cuts were announced, it emerged that Fairfax Media chief executive, Greg Hywood, was paid as much as $7.2 million in 2016 (Robertson & Meade, 2017). This is a sum that Bruns (2017) noted "would comfortably pay for the most of the staff laid off in Hywood's announcement".[8]

The bad news for photographers has been relentless. In 2017, Campbell Reid, director of editorial management at News Corp Australia, announced that most photographers would be made redundant, with News Corp's Adelaide, Melbourne, Brisbane, and Sydney operations each losing more than a dozen photographers (Ward, 2017a). This move alone apparently led to savings of $10 million (Ward, 2017a) and was seen as an attempt to "streamline" editorial operations by "moving from an in-house photographic model to using a mixture of staff specialists, plus freelance and agency content" (Ward, 2017a). Again in 2018, more News Corp photographers lost their jobs at the Adelaide office as part of a voluntary redundancy scheme, with much of its photography work being outsourced to the news agency AAP (Samios, 2018b). Across this entire period of tremendous disruption in staffing levels, News Corp Australia has remained reluctant to reveal the exact numbers of job losses.[9] Therefore, it has been very difficult to provide exact figures on how many remain on salaried positions.

Similarly depressing stories emerge from Australia's public broadcaster, the Australian Broadcasting Corporation (ABC), which has for a long time

8 Hywood's eventual redundancy payout as a result of the merger between Fairfax Media and Nine Entertainment in 2018 was estimated to reach $8.2 million (Grigg, 2018).
9 The *Guardian* did, however, report that, in relation to the 2017 losses, 13 photographers in Queensland were forced to take redundancies, with 25 let go in New South Wales and 10 in South Australia (Ward, 2017b).

(under conservative governments) borne the brunt of relentless funding cuts, and these cuts have also impacted ABC News.[10] Meade (2018a) reports that since 2014, the ABC has shed more than 1,000 jobs.

In 2014, more than 400 people (close to 10 per cent of the workforce) faced redundancy when the federal government announced that it would cut $207 million from ABC's next budget in July 2015 (Kidd, 2014b). A quarter of these redundancies were in the news division (Kidd, 2014a). However, then director of news, Kate Torney, said 70 new positions would be created, with a focus on digital skills, meaning an overall reduction of 30 jobs in news (cited in Kidd, 2014a). In 2016, the May 6 federal budget reduced the ABC News budget by 3 per cent ($7 million), having repercussions for approximately 30 positions and 14 expected job losses (Robin, 2016). More recently, in 2018, 20 newsroom positions were lost (Samios, 2018a) in a restructuring of ABC's eight capital city newsrooms.[11] Director of News, Analysis and Investigations, Gaven Morris, said the current newsroom structure did not fully support ABC staff to meet "modern audience needs". He suggested that the restructuring would result in the same number of editorial employees, as "new senior editorial roles would be introduced to add to the expertise and skills in the newsroom" (Morris, cited in Samios, 2018a).

Even the news agency AAP has not been immune to staffing cuts. It recently joined the fray of redundancies when in June 2018, it announced a voluntary redundancy program – with between 20 and 25 positions to be cut. "Reduced market demand" was quoted as the reason for the job losses (Kelly, 2018). This news came shortly after it closed its New Zealand Newswire in April 2018 (Kelly, 2018).

In sum, the Australian news media market has undergone a dramatic shrinking of staff/salaried positions of news workers over the last decade, and photographic departments at all of the major news organizations have been decimated. What has not diminished in this same period is the demand for photographic/visual material to report on daily news happenings. The task of the research presented in this volume is to assess the quality and diversity of the photographs that are now published in the Australian news media, and to determine the extent to which images from non-professional sources that sit beyond the journalistic remit are now being called upon to

10  The ABC is financed by the federal government, primarily through triennial funding arrangements (see www.aph.gov.au/About_Parliament/Parliamentary_Departments/ Parliamentary_Library/Publications_Archive/archive/fundingabc for further details).
11  Meade (2018a) reports this number as 22 job losses in the national newsroom.

fill the gap left by industry cuts. In so doing, this volume presents a complete picture of contemporary practice in relation to the sourcing of images by the Australian news media and goes some way in addressing the shortfall, noted by Anderson (2014, p. 28), in the Australian literature on current photojournalistic practices.

# 2 Investigating visual sourcing practices

## Data and methodology

Chapter 2 begins by examining the historical shifts in sourcing and attribution practices in relation to press photographs. It then introduces the news organizations that were included in the study and lays out the methodological and analytical foundations that underpin the empirical case studies undertaken for this book. The study follows a mixed-methods approach (Johnson et al., 2007) by integrating quantitative and qualitative approaches in a single study (Creswell, 2003), thus allowing for multiple perspectives on the same issue. This is achieved through a large-scale quantitative survey of the sourcing of news imagery by the Australian news media and case studies on specialist reporting combined with qualitative ethnographic interviews with industry professionals. Brought together, these three studies give multiple perspectives on the massive cultural shifts being experienced by the Australian journalism industry today and its capacity to adapt positively to these changes.

## The sourcing and attribution of news photographs

Attributing photographs to the professional photographer, i.e. the use of bylines, has been a point of considerable tension since photographs were first published in the news media and attests to the constant struggle that press photographers have had to endure in securing professional status for themselves and their work (compared to their wordsmith colleagues). To give an early example from the Australian news context, George Berlin, the photographer who produced one of the first news photographs published in an Australian newspaper (in 1888), took the rather unusual step of painting his name onto the side of the crashed steam train he was photographing for the *Sydney Mail* in order to ensure that he was given credit for the photograph (Anderson & Young, 2016, p. 3). Throughout much of the twentieth century, photographer bylines were not common practice, and as Anderson and Young (2016, p. 3) note, it was not until the 1980s that Australian press photographers were routinely given byline credits for their photographs.

Similar findings were revealed by Reich and Klein-Avraham (2014) in their longitudinal study of attribution practices at major newspapers in the northern hemisphere, with personal bylines for photographers emerging in the 1970s–1980s, but consistently lagging behind those for reporters. In fact, for most of the twentieth century, attribution was routinely assigned to the publisher or employer, a practice that Reich and Klein-Avraham (2104, p. 625) explain exposes the weaknesses of photojournalism and the photographer. They point to key strategies that contributed to photography being viewed as socioculturally inferior to language. These include the marginalization of the photograph in terms of its meaning potential, labelling it as "adjunct" to verbal reporting (Becker, 1992, p. 130; Zelizer, 2004, p. 118), or limiting it to its denotative (descriptive) function, or suggesting that the capture of an image is something that anyone can successfully do. At Gannett newspapers in the US during the 1930s and 40s, for example, suburban circulation truck drivers at the Olean *Times Herald* were equipped with small cameras to "take pictures that were of interest to them", and owner Frank Gannett suggested that "even girls" could take photographs "with the proper technology" (Brennen, 1998, p. 66). Another strategy involved removing the agency of the photographer in the capture of the photograph, a practice that today is commonly associated with the "authorless" images of crisis events captured by amateurs (Pantti, 2013a, p. 210), wherein images are attributed solely to recording devices, content-sharing sites, and distribution channels (e.g. Facebook, Getty).

With citizen-produced images now making their way more often into the legacy news media, a considerable body of research has emerged on the values associated with the publication of eyewitness photography, particularly in relation to crisis events (see, for example, contributions to Allan, 2013, 2015; Andén-Papadopoulos & Pantti, 2013, p. 960; Andén-Papadopoulos & Pantti, 2014; Allan & Peters, 2015). However, there is little research on attribution practices with respect to the publication of citizen images. In relation to the Syrian crisis (2011–2012), Mast and Hanegreefs (2015, p. 603) found that either indirect source citations (to a news agency) or no reference at all was used by Flemish news media when incorporating citizen-produced visuals into their reporting.[1] Such a lack of transparency in attribution practices effectively masks the potential unreliability of certain content. It also masks potential negative evaluation of citizen imagery, as pointed out by Buehner Mortensen and Keshelashvili (2013), who experimented with attribution practices. They found that professional photographers rated images

---

1   In relation to attribution practices surrounding the use of video footage supplied by citizens, see Pantti and Andén-Papadopoulos (2011), Harkin et al. (2012).

that were attributed to citizens much lower than images with no attribution at all. This, they suggest, is based on a "threatened sense of professionalism" where amateur photographers are seen as lacking the professional values of their professional counterparts (p. 152).

The idea that a variety of differently skilled people may be tasked with the capture of photographs is not a new phenomenon. To draw again on the Australian context, photographs have always been supplied by multiple sources. One of the most significant news events in colonial Australian history, the capture and killing of the Kelly gang in 1880, was photographed by "a mix of studio, amateur and freelance photographers" (Anderson & Young, 2016, p. 1). The first pictorial daily newspaper in Australia, the *Sun News-Pictorial*, advertised its willingness to pay for news photographs from "either amateur or professional photographers" (Anderson & Young, 2016, p. 7). Journalists have also been known throughout history to carry cameras and to photograph their interviewees, an example being the political journalist Bert Cook of the *Melbourne Herald*, who at the turn of the twentieth century was known to have photographed cabinet ministers at their desks (Anderson & Young, 2016, p. 297). Since the early 2000s, the Australian news media have begun remarking on the potential for using amateur images in their reporting. Anderson and Young (2016, p. 18) note how in 2004, following a fire in Brisbane, the *Courier Mail* (a Brisbane tabloid newspaper owned by News Corp Australia) used amateur photographs in the reporting of this story. A subsequent article in the same newspaper suggested that "mobile phones would turn accidental onlookers into on-the-spot journalists, taking part in the newsgathering process".

Australian news organizations also routinely present both amateur and professionally produced imagery side by side in online news galleries, which are collections of sequentially organized photographs (and captions) in an online interface (Caple & Knox, 2012). This is especially the case in relation to the reporting of crisis events, such as natural disasters (Caple, 2013, p. 193), as will be demonstrated in Chapter 3.

As the research discussed in this volume will show, attribution practices in the Australian context remain somewhat inconsistent, and when the sourcing of images ranges from the fully automated screen grab from CCTV footage to the highly crafted and technically complex photography of the professional photographer and includes everything in between, it has never been more critical to clearly establish and then communicate to audiences the origin and reliability of the visuals that are used to tell news stories.

In exploring sourcing and attribution practices in contemporary newsrooms, I focus quite specifically on the Australian news media context. The reasons for this have already been outlined in Chapter 1 and include most significantly the fact that more than 3,000 editorial positions, among them many professional photographers, have been shed from Australian news media companies. However, the need for photographs in news storytelling has not diminished. Therefore, the question remains: Where do these photographs come from? This research is tasked with answering this question. The aims of this book are as follows:

1   To map contemporary practices in the sourcing of news imagery by Australian news media organizations
2   To identify the values associated with professional and amateur practices in photography, and assess their relative capacities to bear effective witness
3   To assess professional photojournalism's experience of structural transformation and its capacity to adapt positively to change

In the next section, I introduce the news media examined for this study and justify why these particular news media organizations have been selected.

## The news media in Australia

As noted in Chapter 1, the concentration of news media ownership in Australia ranks among the highest in the world (fact-checked by Dwyer, 2016). Two long-standing newspaper companies dominate the newspaper industry: News Corp Australia and Fairfax Media (Newman et al., 2017, p. 116) with News Corp Australia–controlled newspapers constituting the sole metropolitan newspaper source in four of Australia's eight state/territory capital cities. The ABC is a government-funded national broadcaster that provides both broadcast and online continuous news services. A major producer of Australian news copy accessed by all of the Australian news media organizations is the newswire service AAP. AAP was established in 1935 and boasts more than 600 employees located all around the world (AAP, 2018).[2] AAP is co-owned by Fairfax Media (47 per cent), News Corp Australia (45 per cent), and Australian integrated media company Seven West Media (8 per cent).

Since completing this research project, Fairfax Media has been sold to Nine Entertainment, a publicly listed media company that operates across four divisions: Australian community media and printing and stuff, publishing (including "Metro Mastheads", "Nine Digital and Events"), Stan, and

---

2   For a snapshot of Australia's broader media market, see Newman et al. (2017, pp. 116–117) and Australia Communications and Media Authority's information visualization at www. acma.gov.au/theACMA/media-interests-snapshot.

television (About Us, 2019). Assets include the Nine Network (commercial television); digital properties, such as nine.com.au, 9Honey, Pedestrian. TV, and CarAdvice; and the subscription video-on-demand platform Stan. With the acquisition of Fairfax Media, this now also includes the major mastheads the *Sydney Morning Herald, The Age*, and *Australian Financial Review*. Since the empirical case studies discussed throughout this book were completed before this takeover, I continue to refer to the company as Fairfax Media throughout the remainder of the book.

In Australia, a number of "digital first" news and commentary platforms have emerged throughout the twenty-first century: Crikey (www.crikey.com.au) was founded by Stephen Mayne in 2000, New Matilda (www.newmatilda.com) by John Menadue in 2004. In 2013, the UK's *Guardian* newspaper launched an Australian online-only platform, Guardian Australia (www.theguardian.com/au), attaining an editorial staff of 49 in 2018. MailOnline launched an Australian site in 2014 (www.dailymail.co.uk/auhome/index.html), and the American sites Buzzfeed and Huffington Post have operated Australian platforms since 2014–2015.

News Corp Australia, Fairfax Media, and AAP are the major employers of photojournalists in Australia. As outlined in Chapter 1, Australian news organizations have suffered significant job losses in recent years, and both News Corp Australia and Fairfax Media have laid off a large number of photographic staff. It is in the context of these redundancies that this study sits, and therefore these news organizations form the central focus of the investigations undertaken. As Australia's leading source for news (Newman et al., 2017, p. 117), ABC News is also included in this study. ABC News provides an interesting model for cross-media news storytelling and the sharing of responsibility for the capture of news photography and thus offers further points of comparison to the more traditional models of operation at other news organizations. Guardian Australia was also selected for further investigation, as it represents the most firmly established of the new "digital first" news platforms, with unique Australian content and an Australia-based editorial staff that has steadily increased over the last five years.[3]

With print newspaper circulation in rapid decline in Australia (IBIS World, 2017), Australians are consuming more of their news online. According to the *Digital News Report* for 2017, 74 per cent of Australians source

3 The digital native Australian news sites www.crikey.com.au and www.newmatilda.com were initially included in this research. However, their record of never attributing or captioning images (Crikey) and intermittent publication gaps (New Matilda) and heavy opinion-based writing (both) meant that they do not add a useful perspective to this study on the sourcing of news photography.

their news online and 53 per cent do so using a computer (Newman et al., 2017, p. 117). Online news subscriptions are also high in Australia at 8 per cent, ranking joint fourth (with the US) overall in the *Digital News Report*, 2017 (Newman et al., 2017, p. 24). News Corp Australia's news.com.au ranks number one for online news, with ABC News online in second place. Fairfax Media's top-rated online news site is smh.com.au (*Sydney Morning Herald*) (Newman et al., 2017, p. 117). These figures have been maintained over the previous two *Digital News Reports* published in 2015 and 2016. For these reasons, these top-ranked online news sites were chosen to investigate sourcing practices for the photography published with news reporting. A computer interface was used for viewing and data collection. The online environment also provides the most flexibility in image display and innovation in visual storytelling, e.g. picture galleries, slide shows, multimedia packages (Caple & Knox, 2012, 2015; Pantti, 2013b), which are crucial elements of the data collection in this research project.

As will be discussed in the next section, in addition to analyzing websites, interviews were conducted with key editorial staff who are responsible for the press photographers employed at these major companies. Thus, interviewees represent the same news media companies as described here – namely AAP, ABC News, Fairfax Media, Guardian Australia and News Corp Australia. Table 2.1 summarizes the news media organizations investigated, with information on the types of analysis undertaken (explained in further detail next).

## Methodology: a three-pronged approach

This research project offers a comprehensive study of image-sourcing and attribution practices in the contemporary Australian news media context. To achieve this, I take a three-pronged approach to the collection and analysis of data, combining qualitative case studies of specialist reporting and a large-scale quantitative survey of routine reporting, with qualitative ethnographic interviews with industry professionals. The aim is to yield multiple perspectives on the massive cultural shifts being experienced by journalism professionals in Australia today and to assess their ability to adapt positively to change.

This study sits at the intersection of the established fields of journalism studies and social semiotics and engages with emergent research in citizen witnessing (Blocker, 2009; Allan, 2013; Becker, 2013) and citizen "photojournalism" (Greenwood & Thomas, 2015). Thus, I further triangulate methods by following a mixed-methods/cross-disciplinary approach to the analysis of the data collected. I combine quantitative content analysis (of attribution practices and key themes addressed in the news photography)

Table 2.1 The news organizations investigated

| News organization | Website | Specialist case studies | | | Survey of routine reporting | Interviews |
| | | Australian federal election July 2016 | South Australian storms Sept 2016 | Australia Day Jan 2017 | July to October 2017 | May to July 2018 |
| --- | --- | --- | --- | --- | --- | --- |
| AAP | | | | | | |
| ABC News | www.abc.net.au/news | X | X | X | X | X |
| Fairfax Media | www.smh.com.au | X | X | X | X | X |
| Guardian Australia | www.theguardian.com/au | X | X | X | X | X |
| News Corp Australia | www.news.com.au | X | X | X | X | X |

with qualitative multimodal discourse analysis (e.g. Kress & van Leeuwen, 2006; Caple, 2013) of both the professional and amateur imagery published in the news reporting collected in the case studies. The multimodal analysis also makes use of the discursive news values analysis framework for image analysis (Bednarek & Caple, 2017) to systematically map the visual devices deployed in citizen imagery to construct events as visually newsworthy. Semi-structured interviews with industry professionals who are responsible for the photographic departments at Australia's leading news organizations have also been undertaken. The interviews uncover the strategies news organizations are putting in place to deal with massive disruptions to the employment status of their photojournalists.

### *Case studies examining specialist reporting*

Three case studies examining specialist reporting were undertaken which focused on key events in the Australian political, cultural, and historical landscape. These are the Australian federal election of 2 July 2016, Australia Day 2017 (January 26), and a spot news event: The devastating storms that hit South Australia in September 2016, causing widespread flooding, damage to infrastructure and a major blackout that affected the entire state. The storm was described as a "once in 50-year storm" by ABC, Fairfax, and News Corp news outlets. The repercussions of this disaster were felt by all sectors and even led to senior federal politicians criticizing the state government's energy security policy. The inclusion of a spot news event aims to account for the fact that citizen witnesses who are caught up in disaster events are highly likely to photograph, film, and post their imagery to social media sites (Allan, 2013, 2015; Andén-Papadopoulos & Pantti, 2013, p. 960; Allan & Peters, 2015). Thus, a large amount of on-the-spot imagery would be available to the news media for use in their reporting. Such imagery becomes a valuable resource when access to the disaster area is restricted or limited, e.g. by flooding, road closures, disruptions to traffic flow and key infrastructure, as was the case with the storms in South Australia.

An event of cultural significance, Australia Day, was also included, as this is a highly contested day of celebration for some and mourning for many.[4] Thus, there were both parties and protests, and citizens photographed both. On the photo-sharing social media site Instagram alone, nearly 140,000 images were posted using the hashtag #australiaday on 26 January 2017.

---

4 Australia Day, 26 January, marks the anniversary of the arrival in 1788 of the First Fleet of British ships. To many Indigenous Australians, it marks the invasion of their lands by the British and the beginnings of the systematic genocide of First Nations people. Thus it is also known as "Invasion Day" or "Survival Day", and is a day of mourning. Some groups are now campaigning for the date of this event to be changed.

This provides a wealth of imagery to the news media that could be taken up for publication. Instagram formed another branch of research in my project (occasionally alluded to in this book). Hence I have accurate figures for the number of posts made in relation to each of the events in the three case studies. The federal election stands as a case study where one would expect to find most reporting to be supplied by the professional news workers embedded with politicians as they make their final bids to the public on their voting preferences. It has been included to potentially offer a point of contrast in the sourcing of photographs.

Data collection for two of the case studies spanned five days. As the dates of Australia Day and the federal election are both fixed ahead of time, data collection occurred on the two days preceding the event, on the day of the event, and on the two days after the event. With the spot news event, the storms in South Australia, data collection began on 27 September 2016, the day before the major storm hit Adelaide on 28 September, as the storm front was moving in over the coastline. It continued until 4 October 2016, since there was considerable political fallout in the wake of the storms in relation to South Australia's reliance on renewable energy.

News reporting focusing on these three events, the federal election of 2016, Australia Day 2017, and the storms that hit South Australia in September 2016, which was published online in each of the four news outlets being investigated, was collected manually. I did not collect opinion pieces or sponsored content, as explained in the next section. The websites were scanned for relevant content twice a day throughout the collection period.

In relation to the specialist case studies, all news organizations created special sections (with a hyperlink from the navigation bar of the home page) where the reporting on the federal election and Australia Day was collected (examples are shown in Figure 2.1). Thus, I scanned both the main "News" section and these special sections for news reports on these events. For the other case study, examining reporting about the South Australian storms, I collected stories from the main "News" sections.

A Microsoft Excel spreadsheet was used for data collection. News reporting that dealt directly with each of the topics in the case studies was identified, and then key information about each article was noted in the spreadsheet. This included date of publication, story URL, number of photographs per story, caption to the photograph, photo byline and source, section in which the story appeared, story author, headline, and lead paragraph. Each photograph was screen captured, along with the immediate co-text, including caption, and in some cases headlines, and lead paragraphs if they occurred on the same screen as the image. Each photograph was given a unique ID number which corresponded to its record in the spreadsheet. Photo sourcing information sought to uncover photo attribution practices at each news outlet, thus answering the question of whether a photograph

*Figure 2.1* Mastheads for the special sections created for the federal election reporting

was attributed to a named individual (using a byline); or to an organization (source could be, for example, ABC News, or Facebook, or Bureau of Meteorology); or to both, e.g. "Mike Bowers for the *Guardian*"; or if attribution and source were completely absent.

Qualitative analysis of each photograph was also collated in the same spreadsheet. This included a representation analysis (following Kress & van Leeuwen, 2006) examining image participants, activity sequence, and circumstances, which means assessing who was photographed, what kinds of activities they were taking part in, and where this was taking place. I also undertook a discursive news values analysis (DNVA, Bednarek & Caple, 2017) of each photograph to establish the construction of newsworthiness. A discursive approach examines how news values are constructed through the visual resources deployed in each photograph (see Caple, 2018a for a detailed review of different approaches to news values analysis). For example, a photograph depicting a scene of destruction and damage to property constructs the news values of Negativity and Impact (showing the negative consequences of an event). Table 2.1, Appendix A, lists the news values that Bednarek and Caple (2017) suggest are discursively constructed, along with their definitions and the visual devices that construct each one. A discursive news values analysis allowed me to observe whether particular aspects of newsworthiness were emphasized in each of the case studies.

### Large-scale survey of routine reporting

To act as a point of contrast to news reporting on special events, this research project complemented the qualitative analysis of special event reporting with a quantitative study of image-sourcing practices in relation to the more mundane/routine everyday reporting that news organizations engage in on a daily basis. There is little relevant research available that examines routine, everyday reporting practices.

The large-scale survey of image-sourcing practices in relation to routine reporting took place over a three-month period from July to October 2017 and followed constructed week sampling methods to yield two constructed weeks of reporting (see Figure 2.2). Constructed week sampling is a type of stratified random sampling in which the final sample represents all seven days of the week to account for the cyclical variation of news content (Luke

July/October 2017 Data collection calendar

| MONDAY | TUESDAY | WEDNESDAY | THURSDAY | FRIDAY | SATURDAY | SUNDAY |
|---|---|---|---|---|---|---|
| 17 JULY | 18 | 19 | 20 | 21 | 22 | 23 |
| 24 | 25 | 26 | 27 | 28 | 29 | 30 |
| 31 | 1 AUGUST | 2 | 3 | 4 | 5 | 6 |
| 7 | 8 | 9 | 10 | 11 | 12 | 13 |
| 14 | 15 | 16 | 17 | 18 | 19 | 20 |
| 21 | 22 | 23 | 24 | 25 | 26 | 27 |
| 28 | 29 | 30 | 31 | 1 SEPTEMBER | 2 | 3 |

for large-scale image sourcing survey

| MONDAY | TUESDAY | WEDNESDAY | THURSDAY | FRIDAY | SATURDAY | SUNDAY |
|---|---|---|---|---|---|---|
| 4 | 5 | 6 | 7 | 8 | 9 | 10 |
| 11 | 12 | 13 | 14 | 15 | 16 | 17 |
| 18 | 19 | 20 | 21 | 22 | 23 | 24 |
| 25 | 26 | 27 | 28 | 29 | 30 | 1 OCTOBER |
| 2 | 3 | 4 | 5 | 6 | 7 | 8 |
| 9 | 10 | 11 | 12 | 13 | 14 | 15 |
| 16 | 17 | 18 | 19 | 20 | 21 | 22 |

*Figure 2.2* Constructed week of sampling for the large-scale image-sourcing survey

et al., 2011, p. 78) and is an unbiased approach to sampling daily newspaper issues for analysis (Riffe et al., 1993; Lacy et al., 2001). In this way, random sampling ensures that no one event dominates the data collected and thus limits the potential for one event to skew the type of reporting that is represented in the dataset. A sample size of two constructed weeks is in line with the minimum recommended by Hester and Dougall (2007, p. 820) for the content analysis of online news.

The same news organizations were surveyed as for the specialist case studies introduced earlier. For reasons explained in Section 2, data collection focused on the websites for all four news organizations. Each website was visited twice on the day of collection: In the morning for initial data collection of the day's news reporting and again in the late afternoon when any additional stories were also collected. The survey interrogated the "News" sections of each of the news websites. The focus remained on stories that appear in the "News" sections of the website, i.e. they are labelled as generalist news, e.g. news, political news, breaking news, local news, regional news, national news, world news.

The survey did not look at stories that are opinion/commentary/leaders, or from specialist sections, e.g. "Executive Living", "Arts", "Travel", "Review", "Daily Review". Specialist sections often include sponsored content or native advertising, which is described by Wojdynski and Evans (2016, p. 157) as "any paid advertising that takes the specific form and appearance of editorial content from the publisher itself". This makes it very difficult to tell the difference between content that has been influenced or signed off by advertisers and editorially independent content (Heilpern, 2016). Thus, the study concerned itself only with original news content produced by the news organization itself. Further, specialist sections have, for a long time, sourced images from a range of sources outside (photo)journalistic contexts, and one could assume that such practices would continue whether or not photojournalists are employed by a news organization. It is in the newsroom that the most significant changes have happened for photojournalists. Therefore, this study focuses on the news photography that the staff-employed press photographer would traditionally be tasked to produce.

The survey of image-sourcing practices used quantitative content analysis to uncover both attribution practices (as outlined earlier in relation to the case studies) and to identify the key themes that are covered in everyday, routine reporting. All data and analysis was collated in a custom-designed relational database using Microsoft Access. Since this was a large-scale survey and aimed to capture all news reporting on each day of collection, a database was deemed the most efficient way of collating the initial data capture and subsequent analysis of the images. It is also in line with previous quantitative digital methods that I have used in the analysis of news images (Caple, 2013; Bednarek & Caple, 2017). The database provides a very powerful tool that can be used to uncover trends in the data that may not be intuitively apparent and to allow for systematic comparisons across all of the collected data (survey and case studies). It is compatible with other software programs (e.g. Microsoft Word and Excel), which allows the researcher to render the results more accessible to audiences. The full range of content analytical categories is shown in Figure 2.3, which is a screenshot of the database interface where all data and analysis was collated.

The same initial screen capture of the photograph as for the case studies was performed and key data, such as date of publication, section, source, and attribution text, were entered into the relevant database field. The story topic (e.g. a shooting death) and the country the story was reporting on (e.g. the US) were also entered into the database.

A number of additional categories were included in this data analysis. The aim here was to replicate those categories that previous research has examined, particularly in relation to the quality, focus, and compositional competence associated with amateur images. While not all photographs were analyzed for all categories in the database, all images sourced from social media and attributed to members of the public were subjected to this additional analysis.

The DNVA categories were also included, and all amateur images were analyzed for the construction of news values, as I wanted to establish whether any particular patterns of newsworthiness emerged in relation to the use of such imagery. Previous research has, for example, suggested that amateur images bring diversity in representation, of people and places, and a very personalized, emotional aspect not usually seen in professional photography (Pantti & Bakker, 2009, p. 482; Pantti, 2013a; Allan & Peters, 2015, p. 478). Thus, one might expect amateur images to cluster around news values, such as Personalization, Unexpectedness, and Superlativeness, rather than say Aesthetic Appeal.

Pantti (2013a) also writes of the paradox of intimacy versus distancing in relation to photographs of crisis events. Through their abstraction from the event, professionals can get in close with their poignant storytelling and thus create intimacy with audiences. On the other hand, by being immersed in the action, citizens produce too graphic imagery that pushes audiences away, thus creating distance from audiences. However, Pantti (2013a, p. 205) argues that such "involved participants" produce a "valued aura of authenticity" around their imagery and argues that it is precisely because they "break away from the dominant aesthetics of journalistic storytelling" (p. 206) that they do create intimacy with audiences. I include the categories of "eyewitness photo" and "graphic content" to capture any images that may lend themselves to further analysis in terms of their composition, subject matter, shot type, and construction of newsworthiness.

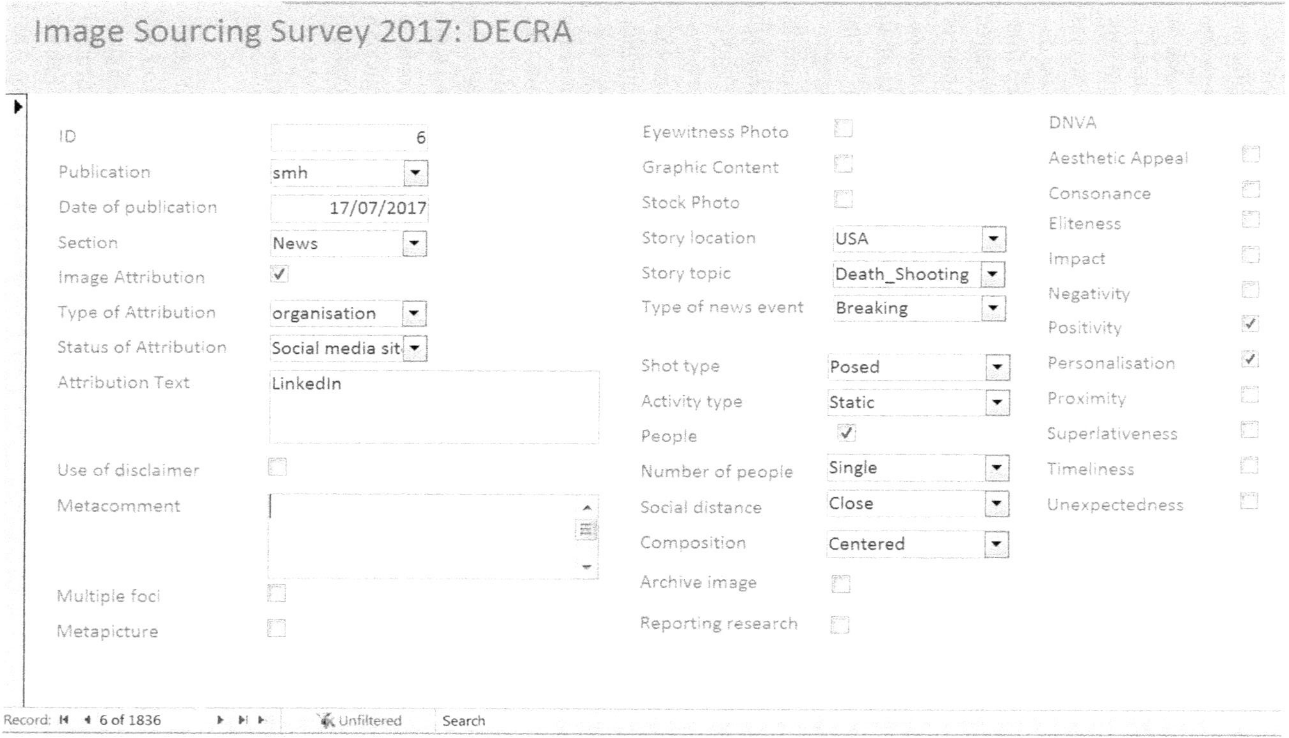

# Image Sourcing Survey 2017: DECRA

| | |
|---|---|
| ID | 6 |
| Publication | smh ▸ |
| Date of publication | 17/07/2017 ▸ |
| Section | News |
| Image Attribution | ✓ |
| Type of Attribution | organisation ▸ |
| Status of Attribution | Social media sit ▸ |
| Attribution Text | LinkedIn |

| | |
|---|---|
| Eyewitness Photo | ☐ |
| Graphic Content | ☐ |
| Stock Photo | ☐ |
| Story location | USA ▸ |
| Story topic | Death_Shooting ▸ |
| Type of news event | Breaking ▸ |

| | |
|---|---|
| Shot type | Posed ▸ |
| Activity type | Static ▸ |
| People | ✓ |
| Number of people | Single ▸ |
| Social distance | Close ▸ |
| Composition | Centered ▸ |
| Archive image | ☐ |
| Reporting research | ☐ |

| | |
|---|---|
| DNVA | ☐ |
| Aesthetic Appeal | ☐ |
| Consonance | ☐ |
| Eliteness | ☐ |
| Impact | ☐ |
| Negativity | ☐ |
| Positivity | ☑ |
| Personalisation | ☑ |
| Proximity | ☐ |
| Superlativeness | ☐ |
| Timeliness | ☐ |
| Unexpectedness | ☐ |

| | |
|---|---|
| Use of disclaimer | ☐ |
| Metacomment | |
| Multiple foci | ☐ |
| Metapicture | ☐ |

Record: ◄ ◄ 6 of 1836 ▸ ▸I ▸*   ✗ Unfiltered   Search

*Figure 2.3* A screenshot of the database interface where all data were collated and analyzed

The inclusion of these extra categories of composition, subject matter, and shot type for qualitative analysis is also motivated by Greenwood and Thomas's (2015) examination of the content/topics and technical characteristics of citizen photojournalism that has been published in the mainstream media. They examined compositional aspects of image capture, such as whether subjects were centred in the frame or if leading lines were used to create more interesting compositions, and found that amateurs tend to centre the subject in the image frame (p. 626). They also investigated aspects of social distance, whether photographing from a close, medium, or far distance, and found that amateur images tend to reflect a farther distance from the subject (p. 626), and produce more static or posed images, compared to the candid, active photography of professional photographers. Amateur images also tend to include multiple happenings within the image frame, thus lacking clarity and simplicity in focusing in on only one aspect of an event. I include the category "multiple foci" to assess whether this is the case in the citizen imagery published by Australian news organizations.

The inclusion of the category "meta-picture" is motivated by arguments made by Becker (2015) in relation to photography as performance and ritual. A meta-picture is constructed when professional photographers take photographs of amateurs (or other professionals, such as forensic officers, rescue workers) taking photographs of the same scene. Becker (2015, p. 452) argues that "meta-pictures of amateurs performing photography contribute to the ritualization of the event as part of a symbolic world in which viewers become witnesses and participants". Such photography challenges the representational power of the practice, and it is interesting to discover the extent to which this occurs in the photography collected for this study.

Finally, this study also notes the extent to which verbal disclaimers are used (e.g. non-verified images show. . .), either in the caption or in the body text of the news story, in relation to the use of imagery sourced from outside the professional journalistic context. This aligns with Mast and Hanegreefs's (2015, p. 603) call to look deeper into whether there is evidence of "concern over the reliability of the imagery" acknowledged in the accompanying text.

### *Interviews with industry professionals*

As mentioned, the third strand of this research project involved semi-structured, face-to-face interviews with industry professionals who are responsible for the photographic departments at each of the news organizations studied in this project. The interviewees were Stuart Watt, head of distribution for ABC News; Mags King, Managing Photo Editor at Fairfax Media; Neil Bennett, National Photographic Manager at News Corp Australia; Carly Earl, Picture Editor at Guardian Australia; and Phil McLean, Executive Editor at AAP. The newswire service AAP was included in this study, as it is a major supplier of news copy and photography to all of the news organizations studied in this project. It is also the only news provider currently offering cadetship training to photographers. The length of the interviews averaged one hour.

Open-ended questions covered topics such as current employment conditions for press photographers within each organization; job losses over the last decade whether through redundancies, retirements, or restructuring; and models currently in place for the supply of photography. Questions also sought information on practices around and attitudes towards the sourcing of images from social media platforms and directly from citizens. The role of stock and generic photography in news storytelling was also discussed. Attribution and the use of bylines was another topic of discussion, and here I drew on the practices that my case studies and survey of routine reporting had revealed in order to uncover why certain practices are undertaken. The role of video in news reporting was also discussed. I was also interested in the extent to which photography has a voice in newsroom or editorial conference discussions. Thus, I questioned the interviewees on aspects such as whether a photograph has a determining role in whether a story gets published or not, whether photography is part of the discussion of story ideas from story inception, or whether it is more of an afterthought.

Given the slightly different role of AAP in the supply of photography to other news outlets, questions posed to Executive Editor Phil McLean were modified to reflect the specialized function of newswire services in the provision of copy to other news outlets. Questions, therefore, also focused on the extent to which APP's role in the provision of news photography has been reshaped by the disruptions to the legacy news media organizations that it supplies.

Overall, the aims of the interviews were to uncover the strategies news organizations are putting in place to deal with massive disruptions to the employment status of their photojournalists and to explore the extent to which new models are emerging around the sourcing of photographs for publication in the Australian news media. It must be noted, however, that while interviews may be seen as an effective way of bringing the insider's perspective to the analysis, they have been criticized for their artificiality and cannot be viewed as neutral (Edley & Litosseliti, 2010, p. 161). As Starfield (2010, p. 58) explains, "Many interview situations involve unequal power relations and are sites of identity negotiation". This means that the interviewees are likely to construct particular identities for themselves during the interview, and this should be remembered when reading Chapter 5.

## Summary of data collected

By way of concluding this chapter, Table 2.2 summarizes the data that have been collected for this research project. A total of 2,968 images were

*Table 2.2* Total number of images collected for each case study and news organization

| | Case study 1: Federal election 2016 | Case study 2: South Australian storms 2016 | Case study 3: Australia Day 2017 | Survey of routine reporting 2017 | TOTAL |
|---|---|---|---|---|---|
| | 30 June – 4 July | 22 Sept – 4 Oct | 24 Jan – 28 Jan | July to October | |
| ABC News | 86 | 153 | 77 | 585 | **901** |
| Fairfax Media | 154 | 36 | 105 | 395 | **690** |
| Guardian Australia | 74 | 18 | 47 | 273 | **412** |
| News Corp Australia | 126 | 194 | 63 | 582 | **965** |
| **TOTAL** | **440** | **401** | **292** | **1,835** | **2,968** |

collected for analysis. This was complemented by interview data from conversations with five industry professionals.

In combination, the case studies, survey, and interviews aim to provide an empirically grounded answer to the question: Who is being given the task of bearing visual witness in the Australian news media? Is it the staff photographer, employed by the news organization to document events of direct interest and relevance to the target audience of that news outlet? Or is it the former staff photographer, now casually contracted, or engaged on a freelance basis, to provide the same coverage? Is it the news agency photographer, supplying both news and generic photography to a wide range of news outlets? Or is the task of visual news storytelling completely outsourced to non-journalistic image-makers whose images were not originally intended for news publication? Ultimately, it is a matter of whether news organizations are shifting away from being news producers towards news retailers (Caple & Knox, 2017, p. 8), or even news aggregators. These questions will be explored in the three analytical chapters that follow.

# 3 Bearing witness to events of national significance

Chapter 3 is the first of three chapters that report findings in relation to the sourcing of photographs by the Australian news media. It brings together results of three case studies examining events of national significance (political, cultural, and historical) and how these events have been visually represented in the news media. Qualitative analysis of image content is offered on each of the case studies. The purpose of the qualitative analysis is to shed further light on the comprehensiveness of the coverage that each news organization was able to provide in relation to these events, relative to the staff available to cover these events. The chapter concludes with detailed discussion of attribution practices around the visual reporting provided by both professional and amateur sources.

By way of introducing the data collected for analysis, Table 3.1 presents the total number of stories and photographs collected from each news outlet, giving a total of 1,133 photographs across all case studies.

A few initial observations can be made in relation to the data shown in Table 3.1. The first is the amount of news coverage produced by Guardian Australia in relation to each of these three events: 92 stories in total, second to Fairfax Media's 116 stories. Guardian Australia is a relative newcomer (since May 2013) in the Australian news media market and employs few full-time journalists, and only one photographer. The average number of photographs per story, however, is the lowest (at 1.5 photos per story). News Corp Australia's online news outlet, news.com.au (see Footnote 1), on the other hand, produced the fewest stories (71), but the highest number of photographs (383), averaging 5.4 photos per story. Both News Corp Australia and ABC News produced a number of picture galleries in relation to the storms that hit South Australia,[1] hence the much higher average number of photos per story for these two news outlets.

---

1 One hundred and seventy of the 194 photos published by News Corp Australia in relation to the South Australian storms appeared in three picture galleries.

*Table 3.1* Total number of stories and photographs collected for the three case studies

| | Case study 1: Federal election 2016 | | Case study 2: South Australian storms 2016 | | Case study 3: Australia Day 2017 | |
|---|---|---|---|---|---|---|
| | 30 June – 4 July | | 22 Sept – 4 Oct | | 24 Jan – 28 Jan | |
| | Stories | Photos | Stories | Photos | Stories | Photos |
| ABC News | 35 | 86 | 29 | 153 | 20 | 77 |
| Fairfax Media | 66 | 154 | 15 | 36 | 35 | 105 |
| Guardian Australia | 58 | 74 | 13 | 18 | 21 | 47 |
| News Corp Australia[1] | 49 | 126 | 5 | 194 | 17 | 63 |
| TOTAL | | 440 | | 401 | | 292 |

1 For case study 2, the local online news outlet, adelaidenow.com.au, associated with News Corp Australia's *Adelaide Advertiser* newspaper, was surveyed, as this online site carried most coverage on this event and had locally based reporters and press photographers.

In this chapter, I begin by giving an overview of sourcing practices among these four news organizations in relation to each case study. I then examine each case study in turn, focusing on specific findings that emerged from the analysis that reveal both sourcing practices and point to the specialist nature of the reporting. For example, in the reporting of a spot news/crisis event, particularly one that was so disruptive to a particular region, one might expect the news media to draw on the imagery that citizens were posting to social media. As noted in Chapter 2, there was a lot of imagery posted to the photo-sharing application Instagram in relation to all three topics investigated here. There were 488 Instagram posts about the 2016 South Australian storms (using #SAstorms and #SAfloods), 6,299 posts relating to the 2016 Australian federal election (using #ausvotes), and nearly 140,000 posts relating to Australia Day 2017 (using #australiaday).[2] Given the massive cuts to editorial staffing at Australian news organizations in the past decade, photo-sharing sites such as Instagram might be seen as a ready resource for the supply of imagery relating to these events. As a result, one might expect to see citizen images appearing more regularly in the Australian news media.

2 Analysis of Instagram posts relating to the Australian federal election have been written up in a number of publications: See Caple, 2018b, 2019.

## Overview of image-sourcing practices

There are a number of ways in which one may explore the results of image-sourcing practices among these four news outlets and in relation to specialist reporting. In order to give a comprehensive account of how these news organizations sourced the imagery deployed in the visual reporting, I take a number of different approaches to the data, beginning from the biggest picture results through to close engagement with each event and how each news organization dealt with the sourcing of photography to report on that event.

Figure 3.1a presents the overall results, collating both publishers and case studies together. This shows that the majority of photographs published in the reporting of these events were produced in-house, with 58 per cent of all photographs produced by *staff* employed by these four news organizations. However, as will become clear as we drill down into the results throughout the chapter, this notion of 'staff' includes a wide array of journalism professionals employed at these organizations, from photographers and reporters through to broadcasters, producers, and managing editors (and even an accountant at the ABC – see examples in Table 3.2). Further, the figure of 42 per cent of all photographs being sourced from external sources may be a cause for alarm. However, a closer look at these results, shown in Figure 3.1b, reveals that in fact, 82 per cent of all photographs were produced by news workers who operate within the ethical and professional standards of a journalistic organization. This includes photographers employed by news agencies, such as AAP, Reuters, AP (Associated Press), and AFP (Agence France-Presse), as well as photographs syndicated by other media organizations: News Corp Australia, for example, regularly sources photographs from ABC News and from the commercial television channels in Australia, Channels 7, 9, and 10. Such a figure of 42 per cent of images being sourced externally, however, does suggest that these news organizations are also very much retailers of news photography, having to select from the work provided by image-makers who are not covered by the journalistic remit of their *own* particular news outlet.

As shown in Figure 3.1b, nearly 13 per cent of all photographs come from non-journalistic sources. Included in this group are the photographs supplied by the emergency services in relation to major disasters or supplied by non-government organizations (e.g. charities), as well as images taken from social media sites, such as Facebook, or sourced directly from citizens. Of the total 1,133 photographs, only 65 photographs were sourced from named private citizens (5.7 per cent), and 15 photos were sourced from social media sites without further attribution to a named individual. Figure 3.1b includes a separate third column of photographs that were

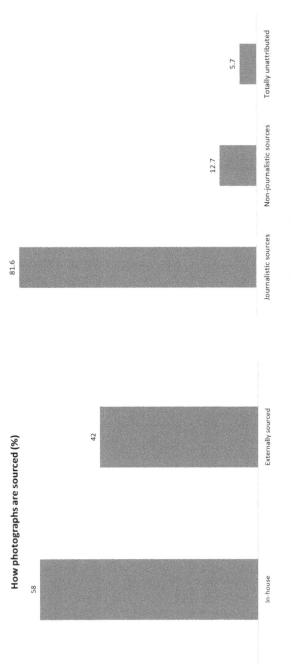

*Figures 3.1a/b* Two views of the overall results of photo sourcing practices collating results from all news outlets and all three case studies (%)

*Table 3.2* Categories and definitions for sources of imagery published

| Journalistic sources* | Definition | Example bylines (From ABC News) |
|---|---|---|
| Freelancer | Professional photographer (principle income earned through photography) not directly employed by the news outlet on an ongoing basis | (ABC News: Luke Cody) |
| News agency | Professional photographer contracted by newswire service, such as AAP, AP, Reuters | (AAP: Dan Himbrechts) |
| Other news organization | Photographs are attributed to other news organizations, both within Australia and internationally | (Fairfax Media: John Veage) |
| Other news worker | Reporters, producers, radio presenters, digital producers, editors (all non-photojournalistic staff) | (ABC News: Stephanie Dalzell) |
| Self-reference only | Photograph attributed to the news outlet publishing it, but not attributed to a named individual | (ABC) |
| Staff photographer | Professional photographer (or camera operator in the case of ABC News) employed by the news organization to produce photography | (ABC News: Nicholas Haggarty) |
| **Non-journalistic sources**** | **Definition** | |
| Artist/gallery | Artist or gallery as story talent | (Supplied: Art Gallery of NSW) |
| Authorities | State emergency services (SES), police, etc. | (Supplied: NSW Police) |
| Citizen | Member of the public (often the story talent or relative thereof) | (Supplied: Mariam Gaji) |
| Non-governmental organization | Charities (often the subject of the story) | (Supplied: Physical Disability Council of New South Wales) |
| Other | Universities, private companies, political parties, scientific organizations (often the subject of the story) | (Supplied: Australian Electoral Commission) |
| Social media site | Social media sites such as Instagram and Twitter (does not include embedded tweets or posts) | (Facebook) |
| Stock | Stock photo agencies, e.g. Alamy | (iStock Photo/Evgeny Sergeev) |

* Sources were verified through online searches using "NAME + Photograph/y/er" or "NAME + News org"
** The majority of non-journalistic sources are in fact the story talent, i.e. the subject of the news reporting, and were verified through reading the story and captions to photographs.

published without any attribution at all (65 photos in total). This group is listed separately at this stage to demonstrate the fact that all news outlets did publish photographs without any attribution. These are discussed in more detail in the final section of this chapter.[3] However, as the closer analysis in Section 2 will reveal, half of these unattributed images are actually professionally produced photographs. For a number of reasons, online template restrictions being one of them, attribution of these photographs has been omitted from the caption space. However, it is possible to trace the origins of many of the unattributed photographs since they are often republished across different news outlets with attribution. This means that, even though this is not always made explicit through a byline, the total number of photographs sourced from journalistic sources is closer to 85 per cent. Table 3.2 lists and defines the categories that have been used to identify sources throughout this research project, and gives examples of what the byline used with the photograph looks like, using attribution practices at ABC News as an example.

Another approach to viewing the overall results of the sourcing of photographs is to look at each news outlet in turn and in relation to each case study, as shown in Figure 3.2a/b/c/d. Again, there are a number of observations that can be made based on the representations of the results in this manner. ABC News is the most consistent in relying on staff members to produce their news photography, with an overall average of 75 per cent of photos sourced from ABC staff. On the other hand, Guardian Australia most consistently sources its photography from external sources (81 per cent). Fairfax Media has a 40–60 split between photographs produced in-house and externally, while the opposite is true for News Corp Australia, with a 60–40 split (external to in-house).

An interesting dichotomy concerns the sourcing of photographs in the reporting on the storms that hit South Australia, including the state capital Adelaide, in September 2016. As a reminder, News Corp Australia is the only newspaper provider in Adelaide, running both the print newspaper, the *Adelaide Advertiser*, and its online portal adelaidenow.com.au, which was the news outlet monitored for this section of data collection. ABC News has a newsroom and reporters in Adelaide. Neither Guardian Australia nor Fairfax Media have reporters and photographers based permanently in Adelaide. Thus, it is not surprising that both ABC News and News Corp

---

3 To be fair to ABC News and Guardian Australia, both of these news organizations published only one photograph each with no attribution. Fairfax Media published 27 photos without attribution, while News Corp Australia published 36 photos without attribution (both tracking at approximately 9 per cent of their total published).

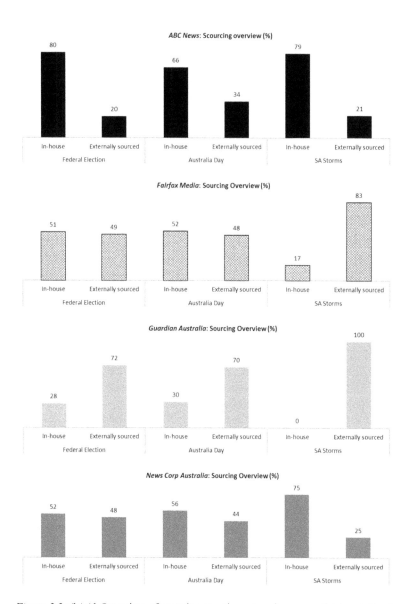

*Figure 3.2a/b/c/d* Overview of sourcing practices at each news outlet in relation to each case study

Australia have produced the vast majority (79 per cent and 75 per cent, respectively) of their photography in-house, while the photography used in the reporting of this event in Guardian Australia was sourced entirely from newswire services. Further detailed analyses of the findings of this case study are discussed in Section 3.

The results displayed in this section give a very general picture of practices relating to the sourcing of photographs by these four news organizations in relation to special events reporting. It is apparent from this overview that quite different strategies are employed by each news organization in relation to each event. Therefore, attention now turns to more detailed discussion of each case study in turn.

## Case study 1: photographing an event of political significance – the Australian federal election, July 2016

The Australian federal election of 2 July 2016 was a double-dissolution election, meaning that all members of Parliament (in the Senate and the House of Representatives) were up for re-election. The double-dissolution was triggered by the inability of the government to pass a number of bills relating to building and workplace regulations. In an attempt to resolve this impasse (i.e. by increasing his party's majority), the incumbent (conservative/Liberal) Prime Minister Malcolm Turnbull called an early election. The move proved disastrous, was roundly criticized in the media (Davidson, 2016; Karp, 2016; Leslie, 2016; Murphy & Karp, 2016), and almost ended in a hung Parliament. And while the Liberal/National Coalition eventually won the election and remained in power, their majority was massively reduced (to one seat). The Liberals lost 14 seats. The Australian Labor Party gained 14 seats.

Figure 3.3 shows that photographs were principally supplied by professional photographers (staff, freelance, and news agency), as well as from other journalistic colleagues, especially in the case of ABC News. A total of 86 per cent of all photos reporting on the federal election came from journalistic sources, as defined earlier. ABC News is unique in that the largest providers of photographs are other news workers (mostly reporters). Also in relation to ABC News, the category of staff photographer principally means camera operators, who are also tasked with capturing still photography. In a total of 12 news stories (across all news outlets), a reporter produced both the words and photographs used in the story. Non-journalistic sources supplied 23 images, with 5 of these from named citizens. A number of photographs, 37 in total, were published without attribution.

It is not surprising that 86 per cent of all photographs reporting on the federal election are sourced from professional (photo)journalistic sources. It is common in Australia for the photographers, camera operators, and

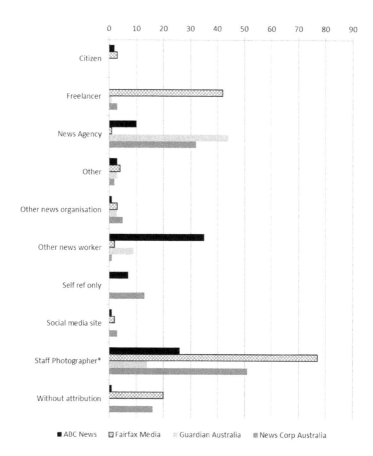

*Figure 3.3* The sourcing of news photography in relation to the federal election of 2016 (raw numbers)

reporters of the Canberra Press Gallery to travel with politicians as they campaign in the lead up to the election, thus providing a ready source of photography. As the qualitative analysis to follow demonstrates, the subject matter of most photographs published in relation to the federal election is largely the political leaders of the major parties contesting the election.

## What are the photographs reporting the federal election about?

To answer the question of what the photographs reporting on the federal election are about, I analyzed the content of the photographs for subject matter (who is depicted), activity sequence (what are they doing), and circumstance (where this is taking place), which in Kress and van Leeuwen's (2006, p. 74) terms constitute aspects of a representation analysis. The subject matter of the photographs in this case study largely involves the political elite. This clearly reflects the fact that the news media professionals were largely embedded with key politicians throughout the campaign. It could also indicate that the political elite are the most important subjects for visual coverage. The graphs presented in Figure 3.4 give an overview of who was photographed in the federal election reporting.

As Figure 3.4a shows, the vast majority of photos show politicians (84 per cent at Guardian Australia) and relatively few images include ordinary citizens (up to 20 per cent in ABC News reporting, but less than 10 per cent in the images published by Guardian Australia and News Corp Australia). Medical practitioners and billionaire businessmen make up the other elites who are photographed as they speak to reporters about the policy promises made during the campaign.

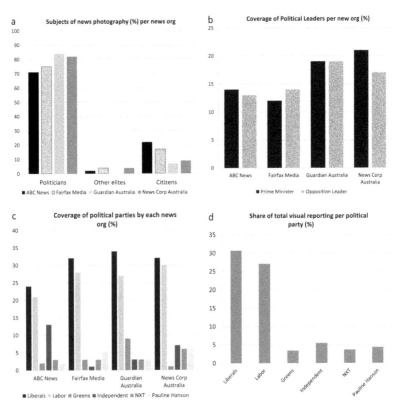

*Figure 3.4* Subjects photographed in the federal election reporting (%)

The two men fighting for the prime ministership, the incumbent Malcolm Turnbull (Conservative/Liberal) and the opposition leader, Bill Shorten (Labor), both received more or less equal visual coverage across all of the news media platforms. The prime minster is photographed slightly more in ABC News coverage and in News Corp Australia's coverage, while the opposition leader is photographed more in Fairfax Media's coverage (see Figure 3.4b). Starker differences can be found in the overall coverage for each of the major political parties contesting the election and in the extent to which members of other smaller parties are photographed (see Figure 3.4c). News Corp Australia gives the least visual coverage to the Australian Greens Party. ABC News gives a substantial amount of visual coverage to independent candidates. Among the minor parties, Pauline Hanson's One Nation is photographed by both News Corp Australia and Fairfax Media, and constitutes 11 per cent of the total coverage from these two news organizations. Overwhelmingly, though, nearly 60 per cent of all visual reporting of the federal election focuses on the two major political parties, the Liberal Party and the Australian Labor Party (see Figure 3.4d).

If we turn our attention now to the kinds of activities that are taking place in the photographs, we can see a familiar pattern emerging regarding the opportunities that presented themselves to photographers on the campaign trail. Many (photo)journalists were embedded with a politician, which means that the photography they were able to capture was largely dictated by the day's schedule (speeches/press conferences, visiting electorates, campaigning with junior colleagues). This is reflected in the results shown in Figure 3.5. Politicians were photographed making speeches, addressing the media, or campaigning. Accordingly, the most prominent news values

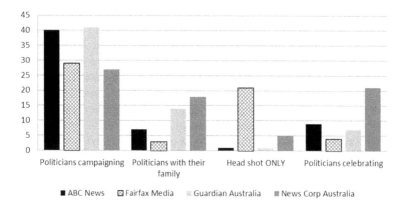

*Figure 3.5* The activities politicians were engaged in when photographed (%)

constructed in the photographs relating to the federal election are Eliteness and Positivity, rather than Personalization or Negativity.

Largely absent from this dataset are the stereotypical photographs of politicians in hard hats and fluoro vests pointing at machinery or "having a go" at operating machinery. Only one photograph of the latter does make it into the dataset and shows the prime minster holding a "hip joint replacement robot" at a Queensland hospital, and is published by Fairfax Media. The hospital bedside photo-op also makes only one appearance in the whole dataset, this time in Guardian Australia, and shows the opposition leader with a patient.[4] Also absent from this dataset are typical "holding screaming babies" photographs. Both leaders are photographed with children, but in both cases, they are family members, their own children in the case of Bill Shorten and a grandchild in Malcolm Turnbull's case. News Corp Australia makes the most use of photos of politicians campaigning with family members in attendance, publishing 23 such photos in total.

Interestingly, Fairfax Media is the only news outlet to make considerable use (21 per cent) of simple head shots of candidates (mostly supplied and official portait shots used throughout the campaign). The use of portrait shots is reminiscent of the carte-de-visite that politicians would hand out in the 1800s (Welling, 1987), thus allowing voters to be able to identify them and engage more directly with the person behind the name, the party, and the policies. Since the data collection period extended beyond the day of the election, this dataset also includes a number of photographs of candidates celebrating wins (34 images in total) in the election. A very small number of images showing dejected candidates also appear in the dataset.

Other activities (see Figure 3.6) that were depicted visually include the act of voting, capturing both politicians and citizens participating in the voting process. Voting, both the act and the sentiment of civic duty and democratic process, was a major component of the visual discussion on social media (Instagram), yet only 10 per cent of all images focus on citizens and politicians participating in this democratic process. The most unusual polling station depicted was that in Antarctica, where Australians at the Davis and Casey Research Stations queued in sub-zero temperatures to fill in their ballot papers. ABC News, Fairfax Media, and News Corp Australia all carry similar photographs of the expedition teams casting their votes (with all of these photographs supplied by the Australian Electoral Commission). Likewise the fundraising sausage sizzles (and creator of the

---

4 Many of the photographs discussed in this section can be viewed via links to the original reporting at www.helencaple.com/research/arc-decra-project/case-studies/australian-federal-election/.

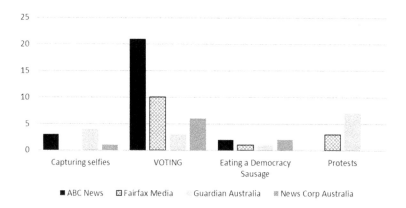

*Figure 3.6* Other activities visually depicted in federal election reporting

democracy sausage) attracted considerable discussion on Instagram, even acquiring its own hashtag #democracysausage. However, the news media published only seven photographs of people (politicians and journalists) eating a democracy sausage. ABC News was the only outlet to publish a number of images (four) of people operating the sausage sizzle. The fact that Bill Shorten mistakenly took his first bite of his democracy sausage from the middle of the bun (!) garnered little attention in the news media. On Instagram, his actions were subjected to considerable derision as well as imitation.

Only Fairfax Media and Guardian Australia use photographs of negative events relating to the election (see Figure 3.6). Fairfax Media obtained photographs of Liberal Member of Parliament Julie Bishop using a phone while driving, publishing three images of her caught in the act. This publication also obtained very blurry footage of a man vandalizing Greens Party signage outside a polling station. Guardian Australia, on the other hand, published photographs of a number of protests, one organized by Greenpeace and drawing attention to damage to the Great Barrier Reef caused by coal mining activities, a second protesting the proposed plebiscite on same-sex marriage, and another protesting cuts to Medicare (national health care scheme). The environment, the plebiscite on marriage equality, and health care were key talking points on Instagram. The act of taking or participating in a selfie photograph also makes it into this dataset (seven images in total). In general it is members of the public taking selfies with politicians, although the prime minister was also captured by news photographers taking their own selfies.

In sum, the photography published by these four major news providers in Australia conformed to the conventions of visual election reporting, and the clichés commonly found in campaign photographs are largely absent. A small number of humorous and unusual outliers made it into the visual reporting at News Corp Australia, where (on the day of the election) politicians were depicted in wetsuits with surfboards under their arms, mowing the lawn, riding a motorcycle, and dancing, hence constructing the news value of Unexpectedness. One politician was also depicted holding a white cat in a strikingly similar pose to the James Bond character Ernst Blofeld (this photograph was supplied by the politician himself to the media). The most comprehensive visual coverage of the election experience for both politicians and the public comes from ABC News. Photographic depictions ranged from politicians out and about campaigning, addressing the media, speaking with the public, casting their votes, celebrating wins, and mourning losses. ABC News coverage also included the political strategies of Bob Katter (federal member for Kennedy, Queensland) through a video still from his smoking gun advertisement in which he literally shoots dead opposition candidates. The necessary resurgence of Pauline Pantsdown (university academic Simon Hunt's alter ego that channels One Nation leader Pauline Hanson) was also captured by ABC News. Visual coverage by ABC News further captured the full election experience of the public through photographs of volunteers operating cake stalls, sausage sizzles, handing out how to vote cards, supervising the vote, and counting the ballots. There are also images of the public voting and the tradition of running the gauntlet through the last-minute lobbyists congregated outside polling stations.

This case study, examining a political event, reveals largely typical visual reporting practices, both in terms of who is photographed and the kinds of activities depicted and in terms of who is responsible for capturing the imagery published. Slightly different patterns emerge in relation to who is responsible for capturing the imagery published in relation to case study 2, the spot news event, but the subject matter remains largely predictable, as will be discussed in the next section.

## Case study 2: photographing an event of historical significance – the South Australian storms of September 2016

To include an event of historical significance, I monitored the news outlets for a major breaking news event that was unfolding within Australia, and that attracted the attention of all Australian news media outlets. On 27 September 2016, ABC News began reporting about a massive storm front that was moving across the north of the state of South Australia towards the state capital, Adelaide. Two storm fronts hit the state, bringing tornadoes and more than 80,000 lightning strikes, and from 28 September onwards, both local and national news media outlets began reporting the storms as a "once in 50-year event". The winds damaged critical infrastructure and brought down 23 electricity pylons and transmission lines. This resulted in a major blackout that left almost the entire state in darkness, along with major flooding and widespread damage to agriculture.

What makes this storm event unique, however, is the political debate that occurred both during and after the storm. Under State Premier Jay Weatherill, South Australia has been pioneering renewable energy sources and relies heavily on wind and solar power. However, as the storms were still unfolding, conservative politicians began commenting on the cause of the blackout, laying the blame for the blackouts on the state's over-reliance on renewable sources. This led to debate and backlash, all of which was played out in the news media over the next week. The case study presented here captures both the reporting on the storms and the political debate that followed on from the storms.

In relation to the visual reporting of the South Australian storms of September 2016, Figure 3.7 gives an overview of sourcing practices among the four news outlets. A total of 77 per cent of all photographs were provided by (photo)journalistic sources, 20 per cent by non-journalistic sources and only 3 per cent (11 photos) were published without any attribution. With this case study, there are vast differences between the news organizations in their sourcing of photographs for their reporting on this event.

As already mentioned and clearly shown in Figure 3.2, the visual reporting relating to the catastrophic South Australian storms exposes the limited reach of two of Australia's news media organizations. Neither Guardian Australia nor Fairfax Media had photographers on the ground in South Australia during and after the storms. They each produced between 13 and 15 stories on this event and used 18 to 36 photographs, respectively. The photographs attributed to Fairfax photographers (six in total) are nearly all file photographs of politicians whose comments are reported in the stories they accompany, and one photograph is a generic/stock photograph taken by a Fairfax photographer that illustrates a story about the impact of the storms on food prices. Interestingly, the first news report about the storms, published on smh.com.au on 28 September, used a file photo from July 2016, showing spectators at an AFL (Australian Rules football) match getting soaked by rain. The fact that the game was being played in Adelaide made for the only and very tenuous link to this extreme weather event and demonstrates that Fairfax Media simply did not have reporters or photographers on the ground near the storm front. There was current news imagery (from both official and unofficial sources) of the storm front available on 27–28 September, as evidenced by that used in the other news outlets in their reporting about

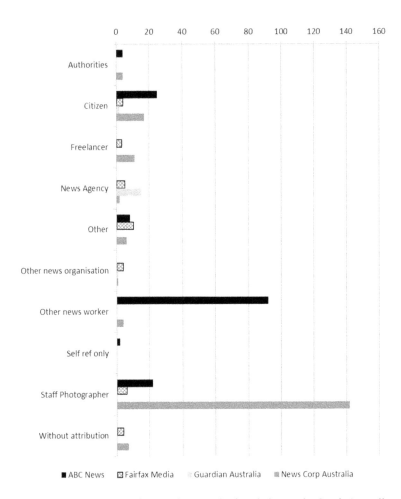

*Figure 3.7* The sourcing of news photography in relation to the South Australian storms of 2016 (raw numbers)

the storm on those days. Guardian Australia relied entirely on photographs supplied by the newswire services AAP and Reuters, and one photograph (used twice in different reports) appears to be a citizen-produced image that had been acquired by both AFP and Getty (more on this photograph in the final section of this chapter).

Once again, ABC News produced the most comprehensive coverage of the storms, with 29 news stories. Like News Corp Australia, it also published a lot of photographs (153), many of which appeared in picture galleries. ABC News continued to source much of its photography in-house

(75 per cent). However, only 6 per cent of this photography came from photographers and camera operators. Sixty-nine per cent of the photos published by ABC News came from other ABC employees: Journalists, radio presenters, digital producers, a news operations coordinator, sports broadcaster, and even from an accountant at the ABC. Like the members of the public caught up in the storms, ABC News employees were also capturing the consequences of the storm event as they too tried to get to and from their workplaces. Journalists and other news media professionals produced nearly a quarter of all photographs (96 in total) concerning the storms.

News Corp Australia sourced more photographs in-house in relation to the South Australian storms than it did for either of the other two case studies. However, almost all of these photographs were collated into three picture galleries, with one gallery containing 93 photos, another 54, and a third with 23 photos. Naturally, there was a lot of repetition of photographs both within and across galleries, with the main focus remaining on the damage caused by the storms. The high level of repetition of content/topics and the random ordering of the photographs suggests that there was little to no curation of the content of these galleries, placing them squarely in the "dumping ground" category devised by Caple and Knox (2012, p. 208) in relation to their relative capacity to tell a coherent and cohesive visual news story (see also Caple & Knox, 2017). More discussion of the content of the photographs is given in the next section.

### What are the photographs reporting the South Australian storms about?

A representation analysis of the content of the photographs published in the reporting of the storms in South Australian in September 2016 provides further evidence of the limited reach that some news outlets had in being able to visually capture the full scope of this storm event. Both News Corp Australia and ABC News, with reporters and photographers locally based, provide the most comprehensive coverage of both the people affected (citizens, farmers) and the impact of the storms on both infrastructure and agriculture (see Figures 3.8 and 3.9). Their photographs overwhelmingly construct the news values of Impact, Negativity, and Superlativeness, displaying the full and extreme consequences of the storm event on the state and its residents. For Fairfax Media and Guardian Australia, the focus remained squarely on the political debate in relation to energy supplies, using (mostly file/archive) photographs of the politicians responsible for these comments, and very little visual coverage was given to the impact of the storms on local communities (as demonstrated in Figure 3.9).

The photographs supplied by members of the public show damage to property (mostly their own) and their local environment. One citizen-produced

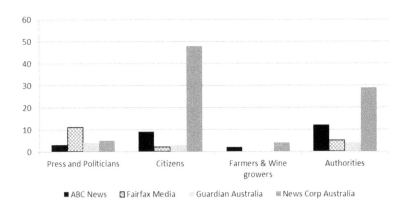

*Figure 3.8* Subjects photographed in relation to the South Australian storms (raw numbers)

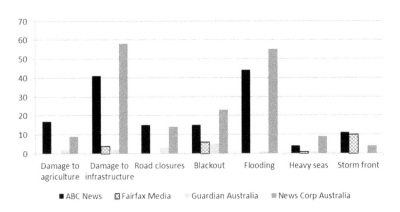

*Figure 3.9* Aspects of the storm captured in the visual reporting by the news media (raw numbers)

photograph, depicting felled electricity pylons, was used repeatedly by all four news outlets and by some largely in relation to the political discussion of the causes of the blackouts. In the next section, attention turns to how an event of cultural significance was visually reported on.

## Case study 3: photographing an event of cultural significance – Australia Day 2017

To capture reporting on an event of cultural significance, I focused on Australia Day. As a national public holiday, it falls annually on 26 January (since

1994). The Australia Day Council (2018) defines it as a "day to reflect on what it means to be Australian, to celebrate contemporary Australia and to acknowledge our history". However, it is seen by many as a divisive day. As noted in Chapter 2, January 26 marks the arrival in 1788 of the First Fleet of British ships and with this the colonization of Australia. To many Aboriginal and Torres Strait Islander people, it marks the invasion of their lands by the British and the beginnings of the systematic genocide and oppression of First Nations people. Hence, it is also known as "Invasion Day" or "Survival Day", and for some, it is a day of mourning. There are now campaigns for the date of this event to be changed. Therefore, there are both celebrations and protests on the day itself, and all news outlets reported on both of these aspects of events on the day.[5]

Like with the reporting of the federal election, similar patterns can be observed in relation to where the four news organizations sourced their visual reporting (see Figure 3.2). For ABC News, Fairfax Media, and News Corp Australia this is largely in-house (see Figure 3.10). However, Guardian Australia again relied heavily on external sources (but still mostly agency-based professional photographers), thus acting very much as a news retailer. ABC News is again the outlier in terms of using other news workers to capture photographs: Only one photograph was taken by a camera operator/photographer for ABC News. All other photographs produced in-house at ABC News were the work of journalists. A total of 14 photographs, across all four media outlets, were produced by journalists who produced both words and pictures in their reporting about Australia Day.

In all, I collected 292 images that were used by these Australian news media websites in reporting Australia Day activities (between 24–28 January 2017). Eighty per cent of these photographs were sourced from within professional journalism contexts (from staff photographers, journalists, news agency photographers). Again, only a small proportion of images (12 or 4 per cent of the total) were sourced from named citizens. Nearly all of the images sourced from citizens relate to a plane crash that occurred on Australia Day on the Swan River, Perth, Western Australia. Thousands of people were already lining the foreshore waiting for an air show to begin when the plane (not connected to the air show) crashed. Hence, the accident was captured in full (its nose dive into the river, the moment of impact, and the subsequent rescue operation) by members of the public. Two people died in the crash. As is now common practice in relation to the reporting of death, news organizations acquired images of the deceased pilot and

---

5 Caple et al. (in preparation) offers a very detailed account of reporting practices around Australia Day, including news values analysis of both the visual and verbal text.

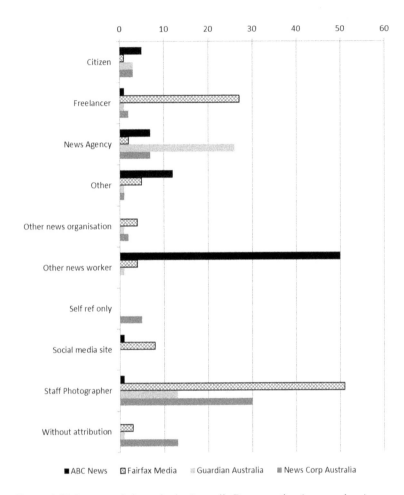

*Figure 3.10*  Sources of photos in the Australia Day reporting (raw numbers)

passenger on the plane from Facebook and published them with attribution to this social media application. In fact, all of the images sourced from citizens or from social media related to unexpected negative events: The Perth plane crash, an act of vandalism resulting from a drunken brawl, and an arrest at a protest march.

Aside from the photographs of the plane crash, no further images taken by named citizens were used in the reporting about Australia Day. Therefore, it may be reasonable to conclude that citizen imagery, including that posted to social media, was not considered a viable source of visual reporting on Australia Day events.

## What are the photographs reporting Australia Day about?

If we look more closely at the content of the photography published in these four news outlets, we can see who or what was visually represented and the kinds of activities that they were participating in. The subject matter of the photographs in the Australia Day case study largely involved elites, appearing in 164 of 292 photographs in total. However, in contrast to the federal election case study, the elites depicted in relation to Australia Day reporting are not the political elite. They are instead local, business, academic, and sporting elites: Most of whom were recognized for their service to their professions and to their communities, and reported on in relation to the Australia Day Honours Awards. Aboriginal and Torres Strait Islander elites are also depicted, both participating in Welcome to Country ceremonies and speaking at various "Invasion Day" protests. The only federal politician repeatedly photographed across all four publications was then prime minister Malcolm Turnbull as he participated in citizenship ceremonies and in presenting the Australian of the Year Awards. Compared to the reporting of the federal election, a much greater proportion of photographs include members of the public (see Figure 3.11).

Keeping the focus on who is represented in the photography used in the visual reporting of Australia Day activities, I also noted the ethnic background of image participants. Assessments of ethnicity were based on the naming practices and other labelling in the captions of the photographs and

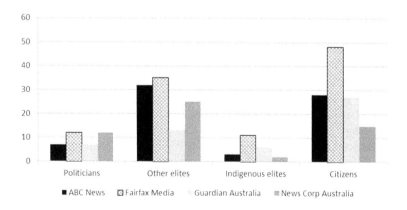

*Figure 3.11* Subjects photographed in Australia Day reporting (raw numbers)

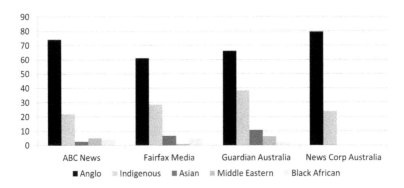

*Figure 3.12* The ethnic diversity of photographed subjects in the Australia Day
reporting (%)

in the story text, not on appearance.[6] Two hundred and two photographs
included Anglo/white people, while 80 images depicted Aboriginal or Torres Strait Islander people. A total of 31 images focused principally on people of Asian, Middle Eastern, or (black) African heritage. The least diversity
in the ethnicity of image participants came from News Corp Australia coverage (see Figure 3.12).

If we turn our attention now to the kinds of activities that were taking
place in the photographs (as shown in Figure 3.13), two patterns emerge
around events that are perceived as largely positive (citizenship ceremonies, Australia Day festivities, and the honours awards) and those that are
negatively perceived (protests, accidents resulting from Australia Day festivities, and debate/controversy in relation to the "change the date" campaign). The most visual coverage is given to the Australia Day Honours
and Australian of the Year Awards, with group and portrait shots of winners
and nominees dominating coverage. Australia Day events, such as the Ute
parade in Darwin, the Ferrython in Sydney, the Australia Day Parade in
Melbourne, and sailing regattas and ferret racing in Tasmania, are grouped
together as locally significant events and make up the second-most photographed aspect of Australia Day events. Fairfax Media provides the most
wide-ranging visual coverage of activities associated with Australia Day
(it also produced the most visuals), from Welcome to Country and citizenship and honours ceremonies, through typical events, such as the Sydney

6 Where image participants were named in the caption text or story text, I also cross-
referenced this with an online search to verify heritage.

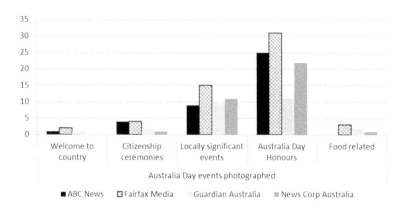

*Figure 3.13* The photographic representation of typical Australia Day events (raw numbers)

Harbour Ferrython and the Melbourne parade, to the quirkier Australia Day activities, such as inventing new ice-cream flavours (vegemite) to honour the day.

A number of ongoing controversial events relating to Australia Day were captured and represented visually in this case study. The most significant of these were the Invasion Day protest marches that took place in a number of cities and which were covered by all four news outlets. Likewise, the discussion of issues relating to the treatment of Aboriginal and Torres Strait Islander people and the debate that surfaces on this day to change the date of Australia Day was also captured visually through photographs of political and Indigenous elites engaged in this debate (see Figure 3.14).

Events that led to death, injury, or damage to property were also captured. All four news outlets included images from the plane crash that occurred in Western Australia, which led to the cancellation of an air show and fireworks display on Australia Day. News Corp Australia covered the fall from a cliff of a person celebrating Australia Day, while Fairfax Media reported on damage to property caused by a fight among Australia Day revellers (see Figure 3.14).

I also looked at the combination of the different ethnic groups with the activities that they were photographed participating in. As Figure 3.15 shows, in all four news outlets, Aboriginal and Torres Strait Islander people were mostly photographed participating in Invasion Day protests and marches. Anglo/white people were also photographed participating in the same protests. However, a much larger proportion of the imagery of white

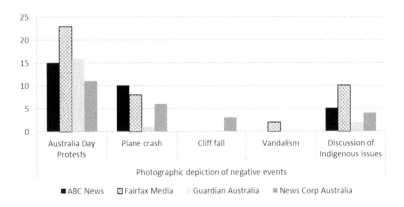

*Figure 3.14* The photographic representation of controversial and negative events associated with Australia Day (raw numbers)

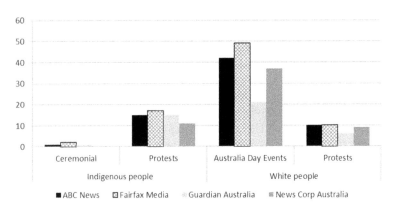

*Figure 3.15* The mapping of ethnicity onto the photographic depiction of Australia Day events (raw numbers)

people showed them participating in other Australia Day events, such as ferret racing, the Darwin Ute Parade, and regattas. Other ethnic groups (people of Asian, Middle Eastern, and African decent) were photographed participating in a wide range of activities, from becoming new citizens (all), participating in Australia Day events (all), and being recognized in the Australia Day Awards (all), as well as participating in the Invasion Day protests (Asian and Middle Eastern Australians).

Attribution practices at all four news outlets reveal that the vast majority of the visual reporting of these three events was captured by journalism professionals, including both photographers and camera operators and their wordsmith colleagues. Very few images were provided by sources outside the new media, and even fewer images went completely unattributed. In the final section, attribution practices across all case studies are discussed in more detail, with a particular focus on those images that were sourced from social media, citizens, and those that were unattributed.

## Attribution practices

One of the ways in which news organizations engage in ethical communication with audiences is through their attribution practices. In relation to visual storytelling, that means stating first who has made a photograph and second where that photograph has been sourced from. As Pantti and Andén-Papadopoulos (2011, p. 102) state,

> Transparency entails explaining and being open about the methods of selecting and producing the news, and it can also include making tough ethical decisions public. It necessarily includes letting the public know where information comes from.

This means that transparency in attribution practices allows audiences to first assess the level of trust that journalists are investing in their sources and then to assess the level of trust they in turn will assign to the journalistic storytelling that they are being offered. Being told where photographs have been sourced from is part of this process. As the interviews in Chapter 5 reveal, transparent attribution practices are a clear goal for all of the news organizations investigated for this project. Achieving this, however, is not always guaranteed, and there are a number of factors that impede bylining practices. Accordingly, this project found that a number of photographs were published without any attribution. In this final section, I discuss attribution practices among the four news outlets researched for this project. I also examine those photographs that have been minimally attributed to social media sites or to named citizens.

Overall, the bylining practices at all news organizations were excellent, with very few photographs published without attribution (65 or 5.7 per cent of the total). Both ABC News and Guardian Australia published only one such unattributed photograph. Fairfax Media published 27 photos without attribution, while News Corp Australia published 36 photos without attribution (both tracking at approximately 9 per cent of their total output). Fifteen photos (or 1 per cent) were attributed only to a social media site, and 65 photos (5.7 per cent) were attributed to a named citizen (52 of these from the storms in South Australia).

Organizations mostly made use of two layers of attribution on a photograph: To the supplier/organization and the photographer (named individual responsible for image capture), e.g. AAP: Dan Himbrechts, Fairfax: Wolter Peeters, or Facebook: Brooke Bethune. In some cases, news outlets only attributed the organization providing the photo, e.g. the newswire service AAP or "Australian Red Cross", or made use of self-reference only, e.g. ABC News, without naming the photographer. The use of just name bylines (without reference to an organization) only occurred when the photographs were sourced either from a freelance photographer or from a member of the public.

In relation to the photographs published without attribution, the only visual that ABC News published without attribution is a still frame from a television advertisement, showing a Queensland MP, Bob Katter, blowing smoke from the end of a gun. Reference is made to the ad both in the caption to the image and in the body text of the news report regarding his win in the federal election, and the story also links to earlier reporting regarding the inappropriate nature of the ad (where a similar still frame from the ad is attributed to Bob Katter and YouTube). The ad was highly controversial, suggesting that he had shot his political opponents in the back, and had already attracted substantial media commentary as a result. Therefore, ABC readers would most likely already be familiar with this image and, even though the attribution was missing, would understand where it came from.

Guardian Australia similarly published one visual without attribution. This was also a still from video footage, in this case capturing the plane crash on the Swan River, Perth, Western Australia, on Australia Day 2017. The accident had been reported by all news outlets and all featured the same video footage or stills. On the Guardian Australia website, a link to the video was provided at the end of the story in a section labelled "Related stories".

In relation to the federal election, both Fairfax Media and News Corp Australia published a number of unattributed photographs. However, many of these bear the hallmarks of professionally produced images by being well-lit, in focus, and well composed. These are mainly the posed headshots of candidates standing for election and are probably the public relations photographs that these candidates would have supplied to the news outlets during the election period. Lack of attribution may have originated with the press releases supplied by the candidates to the media. Of the photographs potentially sourced from citizens, these show candidates campaigning or celebrating their election wins. I suggest that these are citizen images because they are all taken from the sidelines, away from the main action. The candidate is engaging with a different photographer in two instances, and in another photo, there is a child positioned between the main action (candidate greeting citizen) and the camera, which suggests that the photographer was aiming to photograph their child "with" the candidate passing through the image frame in the background. Neither of these compositional choices would be usual in a professional photograph.

Only two controversial incidents in relation to the federal election are captured by amateurs. Three photographs published by Fairfax Media (and watermarked with the Fairfax Media logo, suggesting that they had been purchased by this news organization) depict deputy leader of the Liberal Party, Julie Bishop, "caught in the act" of using a mobile phone while driving a car. While the images are unattributed, one caption acknowledges that they are taken from a citizen source, by naming the photographer as "the witness". This caption reads,

> The witness observed Ms Bishop using her phone for about two minutes during slow-moving traffic in which both cars were stuck at two sets of red lights.

It is an offense in Australia to use a mobile phone while driving. Fairfax Media, by purchasing and watermarking these images, may have been looking to secure an exclusive scoop in catching a leading politician breaking the law. Fairfax Media also published a frame from very poor-quality video footage, again without attribution, showing a former politician removing signage for another party from outside a polling booth. While no reference to the provenance of the image was given in the caption, the first paragraph of the story did state,

> A video has emerged on the eve of the federal election of former Labor MP Peter Batchelor tearing down Greens election signage from outside a polling booth.

No further disclaimer or verification was given in relation to the provenance of the footage. In fact, there seems to be no concern over the reliability of the imagery expressed in the verbal text (cf. Mast & Hanegreefs, 2015). An updated version of the story, published a day later, did include the full video, again with the Fairfax Media watermark, but with no further attribution to the original source. No other news organization ran either story.

A similar pattern appears in attribution practices (and the lack thereof) in case study 3 on the visual reporting of Australia Day 2017. Twelve of the 17 unattributed images in this dataset have been supplied either by the subject of the story (nominees for Australian of the Year Award) or by the Australia Day Awards Foundation and appear to be professionally produced images. Three images have been supplied by citizens who are also the story subject.

The provenance of two images cannot be ascertained from the caption or verbal text in the story. Both concern negative happenings: The plane crash in Western Australia and civil disobedience at a protest march in Sydney. Both could have been taken by professionals or amateurs.

In the Australia Day dataset, ten photographs are sourced from named citizens. Five of these are provided by the story subject. Three images show the moment of impact of the plane crash on the Swan River in Perth. The citizen status of the image taker is again confirmed by the caption text, where they are identified as "a horrified onlooker":

A horrified onlooker captured the moment before the plane hit the water.

Two photographs of the victims of the plane crash have been supplied by a "close friend" (identified as such in the body of the text). Other images (four in total) of the victims (all selfies) have been sourced from their social media accounts and are attributed to Facebook. The sourcing of social media images of victims of crime or disasters appears to be common practice now. Indeed, such a practice may now be considered the digital equivalent to the analogue "death knock", when, in pre-social media times, reporters and photographers would visit the homes of the relatives of victims and ask for permission to take or copy photographs of the deceased (more on this in Chapter 4).

People also readily film and photograph both negative and positive events and share these images on social media. Therefore, a crisis event, like the South Australian storms, would be likely to provide a ready source of imagery for the news media. It is not surprising that more images were sourced from citizens in relation to the South Australian storms than for the other two case studies (52 in total, or 13 per cent of the total number of images in the South Australian storms dataset). Only ten photographs were published without any attribution, and three of these are clearly profession-ally produced images (of politicians fronting the media). It is commendable that so few images have been published without attribution given the vol-ume of images ultimately published, mostly in picture galleries. News Corp Australia published five images without attribution in their galleries, and these appear to be of floodwaters and damage to property. Fairfax Media published the same image of fallen pylons twice without attribution.[7] This photo was used by all other news outlets with attribution to a citizen.

7 The reason for leaving off a byline for this citizen-produced image is more likely to stem from technical/systemic issues, as discussed by Mags King (Fairfax Media) in the inter-views (see Chapter 5) rather than for reasons discussed in previous research, such as to mask potential negative evaluation of citizen imagery (Buehner Mortensen & Keshelashvili, 2013) or to mask the unreliability of the image source (Mast & Hanegreefs, 2015).

Storm photographs attributed to named citizens almost all concern damage to property or floodwaters. Most of these images are slightly blurry and some with sloping horizons have not been corrected/edited before being published. Only one photograph of the approaching storm front is well composed, sharp with excellent depth of field and lighting balance. There is a high level of repetition across all news outlets in their use of citizen images, with seven images appearing two or three times in different news outlets and one photograph of the fallen pylons used seven times across all four news outlets. Professionally produced photographs of the same or similar scenes are published alongside these images, especially in the picture galleries, and are invariably much sharper, well lit, and composed. With much better quality professional imagery available and published, it is questionable that so much poor-quality imagery is still published in the galleries. However, the aim of producing a gallery of 93 images could be to simply point to the extreme nature of the disaster and its widespread consequences. Such repetitive visual coverage focusing the scope/scale of the damage caused by this unusual weather event would, then, construct the news values of Superlativeness and Impact.

The findings in this chapter, relating to how Australian news organizations source visuals for the reporting of three specialist news events, reveal that little has changed in relation to how or where news imagery is sourced. Overwhelmingly, these news organizations continue to rely heavily on professional (photo)journalistic sources for the supply of photography. However, not all of these professionals are employed on a continuing basis by the news organizations publishing their photography, thus meaning that these news outlets do, to a certain degree, now operate more as news retailers rather than news producers. Further, from the findings presented in this chapter, there is little to suggest that members of the public are being invited to participate more in the visual reporting of such news events. On the whole, their imagery is still being used in the same way that it was in the pre-digital age. However, these findings relate to one-off events of specific national interest that draw on established journalistic practices. It is important to complement these findings with a similar study of the routine, everyday reporting that occurs on a daily basis. The findings from such a study are the focus of the next chapter.

# 4 Everyday photography

## Surveying the sourcing of photographs for routine reporting

This second empirical chapter reports on the findings of a three-month study of the use of photography in routine, everyday reporting. This is an area of research that has been largely neglected in studies of citizen contributions to photojournalism (Nilsson & Wadbring, 2015, p. 487). Most research has focused on citizen witnessing in the area of crisis event reporting (e.g. Allan, 2013; Andén-Papadopoulos & Pantti, 2014), and the previous chapter focused on specialist reporting, including a crisis event (the South Australian storms). This, however, does not provide any insights into everyday reporting practices. Given the loss in staff photographers, one question that may be asked is whether citizens are likely to take up the shortfall in the supply of photographs in routine reporting. The aim of this chapter is to offer a definitive answer to the question of who is being given the task of bearing witness in the Australian news media and, along with the findings discussed in Chapter 3, addresses the first objective of this book to map contemporary practices in the sourcing of news imagery by Australian news media organizations.

As noted in Chapter 2, a survey was undertaken over a three-month period from July to October 2017 and followed constructed week sampling methods to yield two weeks of reporting. The survey interrogated the "News" sections of each of the news websites and collected and analyzed editorially independent content only (not sponsored content). Since it is in the newsroom that the most significant changes have happened for photojournalists, this study focuses on the news photography that the staff-employed press photographer would traditionally be tasked to produce. Therefore, international news reporting purchased from wire services was not collected. However, reporting from foreign correspondents (Australian news workers employed by Australian news organizations and based overseas) were collected and analyzed. This is because at some Australian news organizations, foreign correspondents do sometimes file both words and images in their reporting.

*Table 4.1* Total number of photographs collected for the survey of routine reporting for each publication

| News organization: | Number of photographs: |
|---|---|
| ABC News | 585 |
| Fairfax Media | 395 |
| Guardian Australia | 273 |
| News Corp Australia | 582 |
| | **1,835** |

During the data collection period, there was one nationally significant event that was unfolding over a number of weeks: The same-sex marriage debate and postal survey. Reporting on this issue occurs across a number of days during the survey period. There were also two international events involving Australians that received sustained coverage in the local media: The first was the shooting death of Australian citizen Justine Damond in the US, and the second was the trial in Colombia of an Australian woman on drugs charges. Foreign correspondents reported on both of these events and this reporting has been included in the data collected.

By way of introducing the data collected for analysis, Table 4.1 presents the total number of photographs collected from each news outlet.

A total 1,835 photographs were collected in the survey of routine reporting. It is interesting to note that on a daily basis, both ABC News and News Corp Australia publish more news photography than Fairfax Media. The much lower number of photographs collected from Guardian Australia reporting reflects the fact that it is a much smaller operator and produces fewer stories that originate in Australian events.

## Overview of image-sourcing practices

As noted in Chapter 3, there are a number of ways in which one may explore the results of sourcing practices among these four news outlets, and this chapter starts from an overview of the major findings (presented in Figures 4.1 and 4.2), before examining different sources in turn. Figure 4.1 shows stark differences in the sourcing of photographs between the four news outlets. Since Guardian Australia employs only one staff photographer, it is not surprising that it produces very little of its imagery in-house (5 per cent, as shown in Figure 4.1). ABC News produces the highest number of photographs in-house (37 per cent), yet is an organization that has never traditionally employed still photographers. The most surprising finding, however, is probably the fact that at News Corp Australia, only 15 per

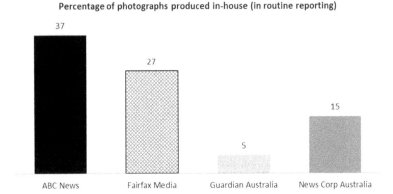

Percentage of photographs produced in-house (in routine reporting)

| | | | |
| 37 | | | |
| | 27 | | |
| | | | 15 |
| | | 5 | |
| ABC News | Fairfax Media | Guardian Australia | News Corp Australia |

*Figure 4.1*  The percentage of photographs produced in-house at each of the four
news outlets, and in relation to everyday/routine reporting

cent of the photographs published with routine reporting are made by staff
photographers. This is a company that has lost more than 90 per cent of its
staff photographers over the last decade.[1] Fairfax Media produced 27 per
cent of all photographs published with routine news reports in-house. Like
News Corp Australia, Fairfax Media has endured significant job losses in
recent years, and this has certainly impacted on their ability to provide staff
photographers to cover the routine reporting of news events (see Chapter 5
for further elaboration of this point).

Overall, the overwhelming majority of the photographs published in routine news reporting are produced by external sources (74 per cent in total),
which is in sharp contrast to the figures presented in relation to reporting on
specialist events (see Figure 3.1a in Chapter 3), where 42 per cent of photos
were externally sourced.

Numbers like those shown in Figure 4.1 (along with those in Figures 4.2
and 4.3) suggest that Australian news media organizations are very much
retailers of news photography (Caple & Knox, 2015, p. 299) rather than
producers of news photography. I use the term "news" photography quite
deliberately here, because while they may not be producing their own original materials, they are still sourcing the vast majority of photographs, 66
per cent, from journalistic sources (principally from news agency photographers as shown in Figure 4.2). A small number of photographs are sourced

1  This is an estimate only and is based on figures reported in Lee (2012) quoting 270 staff
photographers in 2012, versus 10–20 photographers and picture editors in 2018, as reported
by Neil Bennett in Chapter 5.

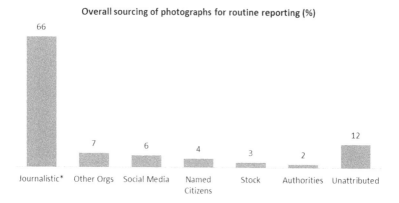

*Figure 4.2* The overall sourcing of photographs across all media outlets and in relation to everyday/routine reporting (*news agencies, staff photographers,
other news workers, freelancers, other news organizations)

from authorities, such as the state emergency services (SES) and police.
Other organizations, such as charitable, activist, government, educational,
and religious organizations supply 7 per cent of the published photographs,
and a total of 10 per cent of images come from social media outlets and
named citizens. These figures are summarized in Figure 4.2. While very little stock photography (3 per cent) is published with routine news reporting,
it is nevertheless of concern that generic images are used in "news" reporting (see the section on image banks for further discussion of this point).
Unattributed images make up 12 per cent of the total, and these are discussed in more detail in the section on unattributed images.

    Looking more closely at the category of "journalistic" sources (in Fig-
ure 4.2), I further distinguished between different kinds of news workers. More specifically, this category includes news agency photographers
(including AAP photographers) and freelance photographers (identifying
first and foremost as "photojournalists" – many of whom are former staff
photographers laid off from the major news outlets studied), and photographs acquired from other news organizations (often through syndication).[2]
These sources account for 43 per cent of all photographs published in routine reporting. Staff photographers include those employed by the news
organization and charged primarily with the capture of still photography,

2 The status of photographers as freelancers, agency photographers, or other news workers
was verified via an Internet search, and further clarification was sought from the interviewees in cases where I was uncertain.

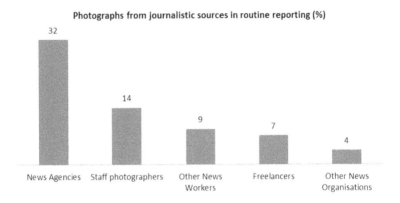

Photographs from journalistic sources in routine reporting (%)

*Figure 4.3* The distribution of photographs sourced from journalistic sources (66 per cent of the overall total) for routine reporting

while the label "other news workers" includes journalists, producers, editors, and presenters (e.g. radio broadcasters at the ABC) who are employed by news organizations for their news gathering and editing skills.[3] The distribution of photographs from these sources is summarized in Figure 4.3.

The figures discussed thus far confirm that, in relation to everyday/routine reporting, these Australian news media outlets are largely retailers of news photography rather than producers of their own original photographic content. This suggests that they are no longer fully in control of the content of photography that gets published with their news stories. Overall, only 23 per cent of all photographs from journalistic sources are produced in-house, while 43 per cent are purchased from wire services, other news organizations, and freelance photographers. This figure of 23 per cent for original in-house photojournalism is much lower than recent ethnographic research examining photojournalistic practices in central European newsrooms, which suggested that 50 per cent of their visual coverage was still original newsroom production (Láb & Štefaniková, 2017, p. 18). For these European newsrooms, the increased reliance on external sources is said to come as a result of the instant availability of visual material online, along with good cheap content from press agencies, image banks, and freelancers (Láb & Štefaniková, 2017, p. 19. More on this in Chapter 6).

3 As noted in Chapter 3, the label "staff photographer" is also used as a cover term for camera operators at ABC News who are also tasked with the capture of still photographs.

Gynnild (2017, p. 25) also notes the increased reliance on news agencies for the supply of visual content to the news media. However, she also questions the extent to which this supply comes from staff photographers at the agencies, or from (cheaper) stringer photographers, employed on a per job basis, or from citizen witnesses. Sourcing images from citizens has not yet become common practice for the Australian news agency AAP. This is confirmed by both the attribution practices in relation to the photography supplied by AAP and the interview data (discussed in more detail in Chapter 5). Phil McLean, Executive Editor with AAP, insisted that AAP does not pursue social media or citizen photography since the processes of image verification and gaining permission to publish are too time-consuming.

Taking a different perspective on the overall results of the survey of routine reporting, the graphs in Figure 4.4 give a more detailed breakdown of where each of the four news outlets source their news photography from. As noted earlier, all four news outlets rely heavily on news agency photography. Neil Bennett, national photographic manager at News Corp Australia, cites cost and duplication factors as driving the decision to source more of its photography from agencies like AAP. News Corp Australia no longer duplicates the coverage that news agency photographers are providing alongside News Corp photographers at the same event (e.g. court reporting). Bennett argues that the cost savings outweigh the risk of having less choice in the photographs produced since both News Corp and agency photographers usually produced very similar photographs anyway when both are booked for the same diary events (see Chapter 5 for further discussion).

Compared to the other news outlets in the survey, only Fairfax Media still makes significant use of staff photographers (24 per cent) to produce photographs for use in routine reporting (Figure 4.4b). At News Corp Australia, more than twice as many images are sourced from social media sites (15 per cent) than are produced by their own staff photographers (7 per cent). All news outlets make use of imagery from citizens and social media, and this will be discussed in more detail in the next section. ABC News is something of an outlier in terms of producing its own photography. Their photographs are mostly produced by journalists (26 per cent) rather than by dedicated staff photographers. Being a public broadcaster, ABC News has not traditionally employed press photographers, although this is now changing (and is discussed in Chapter 5). Up until very recently, the news photography (5 per cent) published with written online news stories has also been produced by ABC News workers who have primarily been trained as camera operators – labelled in the graph in Figure 4.4a as "staff photographer" for the sake of consistency across all graphs. They capture still photographs as well as moving images. Cross-media news storytelling and the

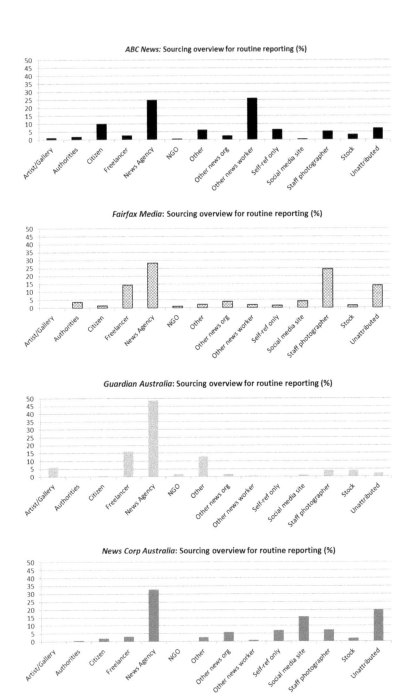

*Figure 4.4* Sourcing overview for routine reporting at each of the news outlets surveyed

sharing of responsibility for the capture of news photography is a practice that has been in place at ABC News since it established its online presence, and cadet journalists are routinely trained in image capture and selection (Caple & Dunn, 2009).

Also of interest in the graphs in Figure 4.4 is the number of photographs that are published without any attribution, which makes up 12 per cent of the total. This number was 5.7 per cent in relation to the case studies discussed in Chapter 3. At a time when the veracity of the mainstream media is being severely challenged, it is vitally important that the sources of all material used in reporting the news are fully fact-checked and verified, and this includes identifying through a byline the source of any photographs published. This issue will be discussed in more detail in the section on attribution.

Summing up this section, it is clear that the Australian news outlets discussed in this research are very much retailers of news photography. However, since similar historical in-depth surveys of routine reporting do not exist, it is unclear whether this is a significant *shift* in how the Australian news media have traditionally sourced news photographs. It is clear, however, that the photography published with the online news reporting at all of these news outlets is not very likely to be produced by staff photographers. In the next section, I look more closely at what kinds of images are sourced from members of the public.

## Sourcing images from the public

The graphs in Figure 4.4 indicate that news organizations do publish images sourced from citizens and social media, with such images making up 18 and 11 per cent of their totals, respectively, at News Corp Australia and ABC News. As noted earlier, News Corp Australia sourced more than twice as many images from social media/citizens than from their own staff photographers. The reasons for sourcing images from social media and the public, however, do not align with common-sense views that citizens will replace professionals in the provision of news imagery. Instead, I argue here that they conform very much to traditions that have long existed in the news media around the use of citizen-made images.

Looking at the social media images used by News Corp Australia more closely, 69 images were published with hard/breaking news reportage. Of these, 55 images were either selfies or portrait shots of the people who are the subjects of the stories, and none of these images depict the critical incident at the centre of the reportage. In fact, their use is the same as that noted in Chapter 3: Being the digital equivalent of the "analogue" death knock, where images of victims of crime/disaster are now more efficiently sourced from social media accounts. As a result, these news organizations are "content scavengers" (Caple & Knox, 2015, p. 299) in relation to the use of "death knock" images. It has been a long-standing practice at news organizations when reporting on the death of a person to publish a photograph showing the person "in life", alive and often smiling. Australian newspapers have not traditionally had access to photographs of the person "in death". And while the latter type of photography is now widely available, given the willingness of citizens caught up in disasters, accidents, crimes, terrorist attacks, and the like to photograph and film the ongoing and immediate aftermath of a critical incident, an image of a person "in death" rather than "in life" rarely appears in the Australian news media for ethical/ legal reasons.

Since most of the images sourced from social media and citizens were either selfies or portrait shots, they are inevitably very limited in their compositional choices. They are mostly posed/static images (78 per cent), with the subject centred in the frame (66 per cent). They are also close to midlength shots (80 per cent) and 98 per cent of these images include between one to three people (cf. Greenwood & Thomas, 2015).

In the News Corp Australia dataset, only a small number (14) of images sourced from social media were taken by so-called citizen witnesses and relate to four breaking news stories. Likewise, images attributed directly to citizens (ten in total) also relate to four further breaking news stories and depict aspects of the critical incident rather than the self. The role of the person capturing these images might be seen as that of citizen witness (Allan, 2013, 2015; Andén-Papadopoulos & Pantti, 2013, p. 960; Allan & Peters, 2015). The incidents depicted include terrorist attacks (in Barcelona and London), a car crash, and the scene inside a grounded aircraft following a technical failure. In relation to reporting on both the terrorist attacks and the car crash, the images sourced from citizens appeared alongside photographs taken by professional photographers who were later on the scene of these incidents. Such use of citizen imagery conforms to the findings of researchers such as Usher (2011) who notes how news organizations absorb usergenerated content into their own practices and routines by filtering citizen content through professional journalistic gatekeeping channels, thus maintaining editorial control over the content published (Singer, 2005; Deuze, 2006; Hermida & Thurman, 2008; Sjøvaag, 2011).

In this dataset, all of the images captured by citizens in their role as witness to an unfolding news event could be said to be of poor technical and compositional quality. They are all out of focus and poorly lit to greater and lesser degrees, and in compositional terms, they tend to lack a point of focus, instead capturing the scene quite generally, often with multiple foci. These are points similarly noted by Andén-Papadopoulos and Pantti

(2013, pp. 966–967) in relation to amateur images (see also Greenwood & Thomas, 2015). Only one highly graphic image captured by a citizen was published by News Corp Australia in relation to the terrorist incident in Las Ramblas, Barcelona. In this image, the body of a person lying on the floor in front of a news stand has been pixelated. In sum, these images, taken by citizens of the unfolding of critical incidents, serve to emphasize the news value of such events, with Personalization, Negativity, and Impact being mostly constructed in these images.

The photograph of the pixelated body published by News Corp Australia speaks to the paradox noted by Pantti (2013a) in relation to the creation of intimacy and authenticity with audiences. She suggests that, on the one hand, professional photographers, through their professional abstraction from an event, can get in close with their poignant storytelling and thus create intimacy with audiences. On the other hand, by being immersed in the action, citizens produce too graphic imagery that pushes audiences away, creating distance from audiences (Pantti, 2013a). However, she argues that such "involved participants" (Pantti, 2013a, p. 205) produce a "valued aura of authenticity" around their photography and further argues the point that it is precisely because they "break away from the dominant aesthetics of journalistic storytelling" (p. 206) that they do create intimacy with audiences. The fact that the only extremely graphic image that was published in the Australian news media was pixelated to obscure the deceased person lying on the ground suggests that such amateur authenticity and intimacy is not part of the canon.

Two other stories focus on footage captured by citizens who were either at the centre of or witness to incidents of road rage in Sydney/NSW. One story reports on a confrontation between a cyclist and a motorist who littered from his open-top vehicle while both were waiting at a set of traffic lights. The act of littering and subsequent argument was captured on a go-pro mounted on the helmet of the cyclist. The lead paragraph of the story reads:

> AN ANGRY cyclist has unleashed the perfect revenge on a badly-behaved driver on a busy Sydney road, capturing the whole thing on a helmet cam.

A total of four frames from the video footage were published with this story, two of which show the act of littering by the motorist. While this story does go on to report on wider issues relating to littering and its impact on pollution of Sydney's extensive waterways, one could argue that the motivation for publishing the story came, in the first instance, from the availability of the footage captured by the cyclist. The second story focuses on a road rage incident in which a man punched a woman in the face. Again the entire incident is captured by a dash cam mounted in a vehicle that was held up by the incident. Six frames from this footage were published with the story. In this case, the story is written entirely around the existence of the footage. The headline and lead paragraph of the story read:

> *Footage emerges of a woman being punched in the face on an NSW road*
>
> SHOCKING footage has emerged of a man punching a woman in the face during a violent incident on a NSW road.

The story then recounts the incident as it is depicted in each of the published images. It also quotes the misogynistic vitriol directed at the female driver that was posted on social media in response to a post she made after the incident. In this case, the story is the footage. If such footage did not exist, it is highly unlikely that either of these incidents would have been reported as news.

In relation to ABC News's use of citizen imagery, a total of 54 images were sourced from citizens. In only three instances are the images sourced from citizens acting as witness to an event. These concern a fire, severe storm damage, and a terrorist attack. The images published with stories about these events are of reasonable technical quality (all sharply in focus and well lit), but they are lacking in compositional competence. All other citizen images are supplied either by the story talent themselves or have been sourced from family members/friends, where the event concerns a negative happening, such as suicide, accidental death, or an animal attack. Interestingly, 33 images have been sourced from the story talent who appear in articles either about their jobs (e.g. a fashion designer who makes clothes for the dead) or their hobbies (e.g. a gliding club in far north Queensland). In all of these cases, the quality of the supplied images is high, both in technical and compositional terms. Further investigation of the sources of these photographs shows that many of them had, in fact, been taken by professional photographers.

ABC News also occasionally sources photographs from its ABC Open platform (https://open.abc.net.au/). The platform publishes and broadcasts stories that have been made by Australians living in regional/rural areas, and is unique among the four news organizations studied for this project in that it not only actively encourages citizens to produce original work of their own but also provides a platform within the organization where this work is hosted. The quality of the photography published through this platform is very high (examples can be viewed on the ABC Open Instagram feed at www.instagram.com/abcopen/). However, when it is subsequently reused with online news reporting, it is invariably with soft news reports, since the photographs tend to be timeless in nature and thus behave in a similar way to stock or archive photography. There are, however, only two examples of images sourced from ABC Open being reused in online news reporting in this dataset. Therefore, it seems that it is not common practice at this stage to use citizen-produced content in news reporting.

## Sourcing images from image banks

It has been argued that news organizations increasingly rely on clichéd image bank material to illustrate news stories (Machin & Niblock, 2008), and this has certainly been the case in advertising and advertorials (Machin & van Leeuwen, 2007), and in the lifestyle sections of newspapers. However, stock images have yet to make significant inroads into hard news or "event-based" news storytelling (see Feez et al., 2008 for an explanation of this category). The trends noted in this book show that while stock images continue to be used, they predominantly appear in news stories that are issues-based (e.g. discussions of policy change or development, stories about changes to banking and finance conditions, or stories about research findings or medical breakthroughs). These are story types that rarely lend themselves to photographic representation and have traditionally relied on generic or archive images (e.g. of corporate signage) to illustrate them.

A total of 110 images were coded as "stock" through examination of attribution, (e.g. *iStock*, *Alamy Stock Photo*, *Pixabay*, *Flickr*) and through their generic content (e.g. a glass of milk, sugar cubes, a pile of currency, hands working a smartphone, hands working a computer keyboard). Many of the images were of signage, buildings, or of objects shown in decontextualized settings. Images including humans generally showed only close-ups of hands operating machinery or backs of heads, and only a very small number of images showed a person's face. Interestingly, a number of these highly generic images were made by professional photographers, as determined by attribution (e.g. Dave Hunt, AAP). It was confirmed through the interviews (see Chapter 5) that staff photographers will also collect stock photographs while out on a job (e.g. of corporate signage, buildings, or head shots of company directors) to be added to their own archives and for use in stories about the economy, the courts, or health news. Overwhelmingly, in this survey, the stories that made use of stock images were about the economy, education, science and technology, health, and occasionally politics, and most could be classified as "issues-based" stories (e.g. policy discussions) rather than "event-based" stories. Overall, the use of stock images in the routine reporting at these news organizations conforms to conventional uses of stock images to illustrate stories that concern ongoing issues rather than one-off, hard-news events.

## The use of unattributed images

A key point in relation to attribution practices is that publishing photographs without any indication of their provenance (be it from a citizen or a professional photographer) may be construed as poor practice. It suggests that proper verification procedures have not been followed (even though this may not be the case) and opens up the opportunity for claims of "fake news". As demonstrated in Figure 4.2, unattributed images account for 12 per cent of the total images published by these news organizations in their routine reporting. The breakdown for each news organization is given in Figure 4.5. The reasons for the lack of attribution are complex and are not necessarily associated with the deliberate obfuscation of an image source. In fact, the interview data in Chapter 5 suggests that the lack of attribution has much to do with technical or templating issues with the online interfaces into which photographs are inserted. AAP's executive editor, Phil McLean, explained that all photographs the agency supplies come with full attribution. It is more likely that the systems that the photographs pass through at the news organizations themselves lose this information at some point in the process. As Managing Photo Editor Mags King notes in relation to the photographic systems used at Fairfax Media, a photograph can pass through up to four different systems, and as it gets re-captioned in a different system, original information may be lost.

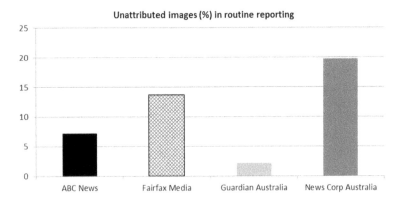

*Figure 4.5* The percentage of images published without attribution at each news organization

Guardian Australia published only six photographs without attribution. However, it is clear in four cases that the images were sourced from the people at the centre of the story, as they are identified in the caption to the image and are quoted and/or written about in the story text. One is an archive image of a famous singer, and one image has been supplied by police authorities and depicts a terrorist suspect after his arrest (identified as such through the caption). Similarly, unattributed images used in ABC News reporting (40 of 42 images) have been sourced either from the story talent themselves or from family of a deceased person. In nearly all of these cases, the generic term "Supplied" has been used in place of any more meaningful attribution. Two stories are longer feature news stories, one concerning the death of a young Aboriginal woman and the other a mental health story. Both stories include a lot of images. In both cases, the layout of the words and images on the screen eliminates both captions and attribution from some of the images, which gives greater emphasis to the images and the white space around them. Therefore, in these cases, the lack of attribution is associated with the aesthetic of the presentation of the story on the screen rather than the source being unknown (this practice was indeed confirmed by Stuart Watt, Head of Distribution for ABC News during the interviews). In such cases, attribution may be given at the end of the story, although this is far from a consistent practice and is often omitted.

Fairfax Media published 54 images without attribution (14 per cent of the total) and of these 32 made use of the generic label "Supplied". These photographs were largely supplied by the story talent or by family members, and a small number of images were most likely taken from social media accounts associated with the story talent. The remaining 22 images were largely archive images of media and political elites, and a small number of images were generic stock images. The highest percentage of unattributed images was published by News Corp Australia (20 per cent of their total or 113 images). Again, the vast majority of these images used the generic label "Supplied". Just under a third of unattributed images published by News Corp Australia were, like with other news organizations, sourced from story talent or family members. Another third appear to be archive images.

Based on examination of the image content (e.g. depiction of selfies and poor technical and compositional quality) and the verbal text (captions and story text), 30 unattributed images appear to have been sourced from social media accounts, and this is sometimes made explicit in the caption text with an image, e.g. "Facebook images show . . ." or elsewhere in the story text. Most of the news stories associated with these images concern very negative events, usually involving norm-breaking behaviour by the person(s) depicted in the images. However, the images themselves do not depict the critical incident. Instead, they are largely portraits of the person at the centre of the story. They merely identify the person rather than retell an aspect of the news event per se and are used in a similar way to those images sourced from citizens discussed in Section 2.

## Concluding remarks

In a similar fashion to the findings in Chapter 3, the image-sourcing practices discussed in this chapter indicate that ongoing, standard practices surrounding the sourcing and attribution of photographs by the Australian news media are still adhered to. Imagery produced by citizens is occasionally used in news storytelling, but this largely conforms to traditional uses. New kinds of imagery that other researchers have noted, the meta-picture (Becker, 2015, p. 452), for example, are absent from the data captured for this study.

The use of stock images by the news media also reflects ongoing practice. It is, however, a practice that should be closely monitored for how and where stock images are used in news storytelling and to ensure that generic images do not come to replace the hard fact narration that news photography has traditionally been tasked to capture. An important finding from the survey of routine visual reporting by the Australian news media concerns the attribution of photographs. Practices around attribution need to be monitored, and systemic failures in how images and their metadata travel through organizational structures must be eliminated. Attribution is important not only for the process of verifying image provenance and enhancing trust in news as a product but also for maintaining a connection to the person who has made the photograph and for acknowledging the value of photojournalism.

The findings of both empirical chapters have shown that there are differences in the sourcing of photographs for specialist and routine reporting. I will return to those differences and the wider implications of the findings in Chapter 6. Both chapters have also shown that it is largely business as usual in relation to how visual reporting practices unfold at Australian news organizations, despite the fact that many photographers have lost their jobs. What appears to have changed is the employment conditions for the photographers who are still called upon to capture this visual reporting (discussed in Chapter 6). In the next chapter, interviews with those responsible for the supply of photography at each of these news organizations give the industry perspective on the disruptions of the past decade.

# 5 The view from the inside

## Interviews with industry professionals

Chapter 5 complements Chapters 3 and 4 by offering insights from industry professionals on how photojournalistic practices in Australia have been affected by the disruptions of the last decade or more. As a reminder, semi-structured interviews were carried out with five industry professionals who are each responsible for the publication of photography at the news organizations studied in this project. The aims of the interviews were to uncover the strategies news organizations are putting in place to deal with massive disruptions to the employment status of their photojournalists and to explore the extent to which new models are emerging around the sourcing of photographs.

### Interview subjects

To complement the analysis of news photography and sourcing practices at ABC News, Fairfax Media, Guardian Australia, and News Corp Australia (see Chapters 3 and 4), editors responsible for the publication of photography at each of these organizations were approached for interview. I also approached AAP for an interview since they are a large employer of photographers and a major supplier of news photography to these news organizations. The selection of interviewees is summarized in Table 5.1. All interviewees granted permission to be named in this research project.

These five participants were identified for their specific responsibilities in relation to editorial decisions around photojournalism at their respective publications/organizations. They represent the full range of editorial positions that impact on the sourcing, selection, and publication of news photography at Australia's major news organizations. All interviewees have extensive experience as journalism professionals, mostly in senior editorial roles, and one participant also occasionally takes on photography assignments as part of her role at Guardian Australia (Carly Earl). The interviews lasted approximately one hour each and all set out from a similar base of

*Table 5.1* List of interviewees, roles and date of interview

| Organization | Name of interviewee | Role/position | Date of interview |
|---|---|---|---|
| AAP | Phil McLean | Executive Editor | 1 May 2018 |
| ABC News | Stuart Watt | Head of Distribution for ABC News | 5 June 2018 |
| Fairfax Media | Mags King | Managing Photo Editor | 16 April 2018 |
| Guardian Australia | Carly Earl | Picture Editor | 3 July 2018 |
| News Corp Australia | Neil Bennett | National Photographic Manager | 22 May 2018 |

core questions. However, the questions used in the AAP interview were slightly modified to accommodate its unique context of production and distribution as a wire service. Four interviews were carried out face-to-face, and one, with Stuart Watt (ABC News), was conducted via Skype. All interviews were carried out in English, and for all interviewees, English is the language of the workplace.

## *Key themes*

Interview questions were structured around five key areas:

1    The first area relates to the current employment/staffing model that each organization follows; their models for employing freelance photographers; any expectations of other news workers, such as journalists or editors, to produce images; and expectations of photographers to produce video.
2    The value of photography is assessed through how it is discussed in relation to story inception, at daily newsroom conferences, for example, or in collaboration with investigative teams. Included here were questions relating to the value placed in securing professional photography.
3    Another area of focus relates to practices and attitudes towards the sourcing of imagery from alternative sources that sit outside the journalistic remit, such as stock/generic images, social media, and citizen imagery. Included here were questions relating to verification and permissions policies relating to the acquisition of imagery from non-professional sources. Opinions were also sought on what citizen imagery brings to news storytelling.
4    Image attribution practices were also discussed in relation to examples from the datasets examined in Chapters 3 and 4, and clarification was sought relating to the correct identification of image authors and their role, if any, within the news organization (e.g. clarifying whether the person attributed with image capture was a staff member [photographer,

camera operator, journalist, producer, editor], a freelancer, or not at all associated with the organization).

5   Finally, interviewees were asked about their views on how the role of press photographer is likely to evolve as news organizations attempt to structure themselves around more sustainable business models.

## Transcription of interviews

The interviews were recorded using an H1 Zoom audio recorder, and audio files were downloaded onto a secure server according to the ethics guidelines given by the University of New South Wales (Ethics form HC17672). Each interview recording was transcribed by the author immediately following the interview. The following sections are structured around the five key themes and where interviewees gave similar responses, their answers are collated.

A caveat before continuing: As noted in Chapter 2, interviews, as a research method, come with certain limitations. Interviewees are likely to construct particular identities for themselves during an interview, and the interviewer also plays a role in the construction of meaning (Starfield, 2010, p. 58). Therefore, the following results should be read with this in mind.

## Key findings

As noted in Chapters 1 and 2, the scale of redundancies over the last decade among staff-employed press photographers at Australia's major news organizations has been staggering. From 2012 onwards, the Redundancy Timeline (www.newbeatsblog.com/redundancy-timeline/) produced by the New Beats project has been collating reporting on the ongoing restructuring and loss of editorial positions at Australian news outlets. Overall, more than 3,000 journalism positions have been made redundant since the New Beats project began collating these reports, with most of the redundancies coming from Fairfax Media and News Corp Australia (New Beats, 2017). In light of these massive changes, I first elicited from the interviewees a picture of the current staffing models at each of the news organizations in this study.

## What remains after a decade of redundancies?

### Fairfax Media

In 2018, Fairfax Media had nine photographers on staff (plus one on maternity leave) servicing both the *Sydney Morning Herald* and sister national publication the *Australian Financial Review*. Four of these staff photographers are female. Also in 2018, for the first time in 11 ½ years, Fairfax Media hired a new junior photographer.[1] Ongoing arrangements with wire services have resulted in the outsourcing of all court reporting photography to AAP, along with all sports photography. As Mags King, managing photo editor, put it, this has left *Fairfax* with a young, fit, and manageable team of dedicated professional photographers.

When asked about how a potential shortfall in the supply of photography is met at Fairfax Media, King explained that this now comes through a mix of subscriptions to wire services, principally via AAP (and with that AP and EPA – European Pressphoto Agency), which is also tasked with catering to the regions and to cover Fairfax's provincial newspapers (at APN News & Media, rebranded as "Here, There & Everywhere" – prior to takeover from Nine Entertainment), and from ex-Fairfax photographers employed on casual daily rates. For a short time, Fairfax Media entered into a deal with Getty Images, who funded a photo editor to sit at the Fairfax office in Sydney, managing 21 shifts per week with photography supplied by both Getty and Fairfax photographers. A major round of redundancies in 2017 put an end to this arrangement, and all ties to Getty have now ceased. In 2018, Fairfax Media routinely called on former staff photographers, mainly from Fairfax and Getty, to file photographs for publication. These photographers are paid casual daily rates for their work.

Another casualty of the 2017 redundancies at Fairfax Media was video.[2] King explained that the quality of still photography produced by the photographers was suffering since they were trying to capture moving images as well. Thus, there was a return to more traditional divisions, and photographers are not expected to produce video anymore. In follow-up email correspondence with Mags King in January 2019, she stated that it was too early to tell whether the takeover of Fairfax Media by Nine Entertainment is likely to impact on staffing models for the provision of photography to the mastheads and online news portals.

### News Corp Australia

As noted in Chapter 1, News Corp Australia has remained reluctant to reveal the exact numbers of job losses across the organization. This means it has

---

1 According to Anderson and Young (2016, p. 295), in its heyday in the 1970s, the *Sydney Morning Herald* employed 32 graded photographers and 6 cadets. They also quote Bodey and Ackerman (2014), stating that after the 2014 job losses, there were only five photographers remaining in Sydney servicing a range of Fairfax outlets (Anderson & Young, 2016, p. 295).
2 While this shift away from producing video occurs when news organizations began turning away from video more generally (Moore, 2017; Banikarim, 2017; Hazard Owen, 2018), I did not at the time of the interview pursue this line of enquiry any further.

been very difficult to provide exact figures on how many remain on staff in tenured positions. When asked about current staffing models at News Corp Australia, National Photographic Manager Neil Bennett explained that the company now works with a core of highly skilled and versatile staff of ten to 20 photographers and picture editors who work on quality exclusive photography for each masthead. Bennett stated, "A much better investment of staff photographers' time and skills is in getting exclusive high quality photography for our newspapers and subscription-based web stories". In fact, quite a traditional model still operates at News Corp with photographers accompanying journalists when covering a story, an overnight photographer supplying hard spot news, and an early morning photographer covering morning breaking news. All photographers are employed by a metro or regional masthead (including the daily and Sunday papers in Sydney, Melbourne, Brisbane, and Adelaide, and at regional papers in Geelong, Darwin, Gold Coast, Hobart, Townsville, and Cairns). The online portal news.com. au picks up and publishes photography from these photographers through its internal systems. A number of picture desk staff are women (also former staff photographers). The *Daily Telegraph* picture desk – the largest in the country – is led by Picture Editor Nicola Gibson, and her deputy is Kristi Miller. The deputy in Adelaide is Cathy Davis, and in Melbourne, the *Herald Sun* has experienced editors Kylie Else and Mariko Nissen on the picture desk.

Like Fairfax Media, News Corp Australia has outsourced community newspaper operations to AAP, and some former News Corp photographers are employed on casual daily freelance shifts at community newspapers. Other newswire services (AFP, AP, EPA, Getty, Reuters) continue to supply news photography through ongoing subscriptions. The doubling up of News Corp and AAP photographers on regular diarized work (e.g. covering the courts) has ceased, and such work is now being covered exclusively by agency photographers. As Bennett explained, while this may lead to the perception that we are getting less choice in the photography that we are able to publish, having two photographers standing next to each other shooting a job results in very similar photographs anyway. A much better investment of staff photographers' time and skills is in getting exclusive photography for subscription-based stories. No expectations are placed on journalists at News Corp to take photographs, although there are some who are keen to learn. Some journalists do shoot video while out on a job or use applications such as Facebook Live for live video streaming. With the majority of former News Corp photographers now working as freelancers, Bennett explained that the company worked very hard to assist exiting staff with this transition. Many of the photographers were helped to transition to the small business/freelance world, and many are still commissioned by the newspapers as freelance photographers.

*ABC News*

As a public broadcaster first and foremost, ABC News follows a very different staffing model to the print news organizations. In the past, still photography has not constituted part of the staffing make-up at ABC News, thus no one has been solely responsible for the capture of photographs. In 2018, however, ABC News did hire its first dedicated photographer in recognition of the growing importance of visual journalism to the suite of storytelling options. Nevertheless, there is an expectation of this photographer to be equipped with a broad set of skills, including writing. Camera operators have increasingly been tasked with the capture of still as well as moving images. ABC News did also employ a photo editor who has a photography background and who occasionally photographed events local to Brisbane, but he has since left in one of the redundancy rounds. As the empirical studies in Chapters 3 and 4 have also shown, key contributors to the capture of photographs have been journalists, who now have photography built into their skills set. This has proved to be a "mixed economy" in Stuart Watt's words, head of distribution for ABC News. Some journalists find it very challenging to try to also capture images while conducting interviews and gathering information. Others thrive and enjoy the creativity in taking photographs. Jane Cowan, for example, is a former US correspondent who after her term there stayed on in the US to undertake a photojournalism course. She now works as a photojournalist out of the Victorian newsroom, producing high-quality photo essays (words and pictures) for ABC News. It is still the case, however, that a team of news workers with a range of skills will work together on important/breaking news stories.

As Chapters 3 and 4 confirm, ABC News attempts to keep as much of its news storytelling as possible in-house. As Watt explained, it is rare to need to rely on freelance photographers for visual storytelling at ABC News. However, there is no question that a professional photographer will be employed on jobs that offer the opportunity to capture spectacular visuals, as well as on challenging jobs where the skill of the photographer comes to the fore in capturing the right moment. One of the aims of the digital newsroom in Brisbane has been to become a centre of innovation and excellence in emerging storytelling techniques. Watt explains that the team in Brisbane has been experimenting with new methods, which it then iterates and consolidates into repeatable processes that can be operationalized throughout the organization. Two levels of training courses on digital photography for journalists have been implemented on image and video capture through to more advanced digital photography training. Such courses are run by established camera operators like Matt Roberts. This means that the ABC is working towards increasing the skills set within the organization, thus reducing the need to source content from elsewhere. This has resulted in the emergence of specialist digital journalists, like Jane Cowan and Jack Fisher, who are further supported by innovation in story formats: Introducing more white space to the page, single column text, removing the sidebar, captions and image attribution, and introducing video and other multimedia for a more immersive reading experience.[3] By embedding such specialists with other editorial teams, the types of content needed for digital storytelling could be fully explored and exploited in the interests of telling the best story for the platform.

## Guardian Australia

For Guardian Australia, a newcomer to the Australian news media landscape, entering the market as a "digital first" platform has afforded it the opportunity to build up a quorum of staff from point zero. However, the number of full-time staff positions still remains very low. Guardian Australia is the smallest outfit, and in 2018, it employed two photographers on salaried positions. These two staff members are Carly Earl, as picture editor/photographer, and former Fairfax Media managing photo editor/photographer Mike Bowers, who is principally based in the Canberra Press Gallery for the sitting weeks of Parliament. At other times, he is "photographer-at-large", filing stories from regional, rural, and remote areas of the country. Carly Earl is principally based in the Sydney office, overseeing photographic operations and managing the production of photo essays and galleries for the online site. She does occasionally produce the photography for longer feature articles, especially for stories within New South Wales.

Being such a small operator, Guardian Australia regularly makes use of agency photography (e.g. from AAP, AFP, AP, Getty, Reuters). It also employs freelance photographers for Guardian-commissioned photography assignments. In such cases, photographers are hired for the duration of the assignment; they retain the copyright of their photographs, but with an exclusivity period for their use on the Guardian Australia website. When photographers approach Guardian Australia with a story idea, a rate is negotiated to similarly purchase the content for a certain period of time. In such cases, the package may consist of just photographs or could include words as well. There are no expectations of journalists at Guardian Australia to take photographs. However, like at other news organizations, some

---

3 An example of one such story was captured in the 2017 sourcing survey, reported on in Chapter 4, with photography by Jack Fisher. The story can be viewed here: www.abc.net.au/news/2017-10-16/jeff-horn-the-making-of-a-champion/9037904.

journalists are also keen photographers, e.g. Helen Davidson. Her photography work features in the findings reported on in Chapters 3 and 4, and those findings also show that journalists working in the regions and other metropolitan cities, e.g. Melbourne, do regularly supply images for publication with their words.

### *Australian Associated Press (AAP)*

For news agencies, speed and credibility are essential elements of their business models, and this is similarly the case for AAP. As Phil McLean, executive editor for AAP, explained, news agencies absolutely rely on speed to market, and getting the photograph to market as quickly as possible is a large part of the value to clients. Also vital is the fundamental quality of the photograph. AAP photographers are tasked with capturing real life, i.e. reportage style photography, not constructed or staged images. Photographers shoot what is in front of them with no orchestration of the image.

In 2018, the news agency AAP employed 15 staff photographers, three of whom are female, and have expanded since May 2017, when four experienced news photographers were taken on (from freelance positions with other agencies) along with four new trainees (two female and two male), who, McLean explained, were part of AAP's plans for "investing in the future". Trainees spend one day a week shadowing senior photographers and then get an opportunity to talk about the assignments and their photographs with photography/editorial staff. As well as providing a standard newswire news gathering service, with photographers based in Sydney, Brisbane, Melbourne, and Adelaide, AAP has a bespoke contract with News Corp Australia for the provision of the photography published in News Corp Australia's community newspapers in all cities, as well as across their metropolitan newspapers in Brisbane and Adelaide. News Corp Australia also assigns a number of diary jobs to AAP, who then staff these positions. McLean describes another client, Fairfax Media, as an "enthusiastic user" of AAP photography. The mix of photography supplied to Fairfax Media is approximately 40 per cent sports and 60 per cent general news.

AAP also employs between 80 and 90 contract photographers who are based in all major cities across Australia.[4] As independent contractors, these photographers do get regular work and are paid a daily rate ($350 in 2018), while specialist contract photographers (e.g. sports photographers) attract higher rates of pay. Attempts were made five to six years ago to experiment

---

4 Phil McLean explained that 160 photographers were interviewed when setting up this pool of 80–90 photographers.

with photographers capturing video, but this failed. Instead, AAP runs a dedicated team of eight videographers in a separate video department, which is supplemented by journalists opportunistically capturing video on smartphones (typically at the courts). No training in video editing or production is given to trainee journalists, and the capture of images never takes priority over the filing of words. Indeed, the production of visuals and words are seen as distinct disciplines, and attempts to mentor photographers into writing have had very limited success.

## The value of the press photograph

Through the interviews, I was keen to learn to what extent photography and visual storytelling have a voice in the newsroom, whether visuals are talked about at story inception, both in terms of how integral they are to storytelling, and whether this is backed up by the willingness to pay for it. As noted in Chapters 1 and 2, photographers and picture editors have long been aware of the desire to showcase great photography in news storytelling, but in recent times, this has not been backed up with the willingness to respectfully remunerate photographers for this work. All the editors interviewed for this project were unanimous in stating that their news organizations do want to have the best photography available for their stories. However, they each have experienced varying degrees of commitment to providing them with the resources they need to support this.

Award-winning photography is at the top of the wish list for any news organization, including at Fairfax Media. However, lines of communication appear to be rather sketchy in relation to photography at this news organization. King lamented the need to continually sell opportunities for photography to editorial colleagues, some of whom simply cannot conceptualize where and how photographers should be assigned to stories, or are too stressed to remember to book a photographer for an assignment. King believes that there is a lost opportunity here in that the knowledge and expertise of her and her staff could be put to better use in guiding which stories on the news list would make for great visual stories. Quite the opposite is the case at News Corp Australia. Bennett explained that how to get the best pictures is central to daily discussions and that it is never about getting it cheap or for free. At the mastheads, a story will be held back until they get the images they want for it, while in relation to longer investigative pieces, journalists begin with their forensic digging into the story, and conversations about the photography for that story will come at a later stage in the development of the story.

Being such a small operator, Carly Earl at Guardian Australia has relative autonomy in the decisions around photography selection and is realistic about the limitations she has to work with in the supply of photographs for routine reporting. While agency photography makes up a large percentage of this routine work, Earl explained that there is strong investment in image-driven stories where the opportunity to produce quality photography is high. At ABC News, photography needs are discussed at the point of commissioning a story, but Watt did concede that occasionally a story will slip through the net. At AAP, much of the day-to-day coverage is diary driven (85 per cent), and as such, most resources are allocated to scheduled coverage with a commitment to supplying a photograph with every significant story. The cost of this work is not discussed at all. However, costs do come into the discussion when longer, remote assignments are pitched, as these jobs require a photographer to be away for a length of time, and their position would need to be covered while away. The value of producing longer in-depth assignments is also weighed against client values and needs.

## Sourcing images from alternative/non-professional channels

As shown in Chapters 3 and 4, all news organizations in this study do, to a lesser or greater degree, source images from organizations and individuals that sit outside the journalistic remit. This includes stock/generic images and social media imagery. My questions here focused on uncovering the circumstances in which such imagery would be considered for publication and how processes of verification, permissions, and payment for this imagery are carried out.

Similar practices are followed at ABC News, Fairfax Media, and News Corp Australia with regard to the use of stock or generic images. Stock imagery is used when there are no visuals available for an online story, or if there is a legal or sensitivity issue with the photography associated with a story. This concurs with the assumption that digital storytelling lives or dies by the imagery that accompanies it, meaning that a generic but visually appealing image illustrating a story is better than no image at all. On the Guardian Australia app, the use of stock images appears to be driven by design factors as well, where images are part of the page/section design (Knox, 2019). As Earl explained, on more generic stories, e.g. cocktails of the week, the tiled home page interface (on the Guardian app) might make use of a stock image (e.g. of a cocktail) to visually enhance the throw to the story page. Both Bennett and King insisted that the print mastheads are much less likely to use stock imagery to illustrate a story, as there is still a passion to use great live photography in print.

At the news agency AAP, the capture of stock images is seen as a second-tier undertaking. Nothing stands in the way of news, and getting news photography published onto the wire is the number-one priority. Preview stories (e.g. of a court hearing scheduled for that day) that are released early in the morning may initially go out with a stock or archive image, but this imagery will be replaced as soon as the photographers file their photographs live from the event. McLean also explained that, if a photographer is at a corporate event (e.g. an Annual General Meeting), then he or she will first shoot the news value of that event but may also shoot some stock imagery of board members, logos, buildings, etc., if time allows. Such practices appear to have become routine for all staff photographers at these Australian news organizations as a means of furnishing their archives.

Social media is seen as a powerful tool by all of the news organizations, especially for breaking news. All agree that when citizens witness an important event and choose to photograph that event, this may constitute the best imagery for a story when going to press. Social media are also accessed to provide head shots of people who have died or who are involved in criminal activity. All have similar verification processes, including accessing GeoTagged metadata associated with social media posts/images, cross-referencing with other (social) media, identifying anyone represented in an image, and contacting the person who has produced the image. Some also use digital tools to assess whether an image has been manipulated or to assess the date of production of an image. Permission to publish is always sought. None of the news organizations said that they would offer payment for an image sourced from social media/citizens. However, they did concede that payment may be negotiated if asked for.

## The quality of images sourced from alternative channels

While Guardian Australia does not publish many social media images, Earl explained that when they do, it will be because the image shows something creative, intimate, or important to the story – an angle that other images have missed. Further, rather than take it down when more professionally produced photographs become available, Earl stated that photographs that captured different aspects of the story would be added. King added that there is an urgency to citizen images: They lack the artistry we expect from professional photography, but they may still capture the essence of an event. Bennett believes that these are exciting times for photography, with smartphone users now much more educated about how to capture images and what the technology affords. Rather than displace traditional photography, he believes, citizen contributions could lead to a multiplication of visual storytelling, bringing out alternative facets of the story while also experimenting with technical aspects, such as using filters or shooting into light (cf. Nilsson & Wadbring, 2015, p. 496).

## Attribution practices

Crediting the photographer and publisher of photographs used by the Australian news media is generally very consistent, as names, agencies, captions, and other metadata usually travel with a photograph through the systems and databases that each organization uses. Sometimes, however, these systems fail, or are incompatible with each other, and such information is lost. This is how the interviewees explained the use of the generic label "Supplied" in place of named attribution with published images. Another reason for using this label is for privacy or legal reasons, or if naming the photographer might put them in harm's way. Earl explained that when Guardian Australia may wish to publish images exposing a wrongdoing or untenable conditions (e.g. concerning the conditions in which refugees on Manus Island are being held), then she would most likely use the term "Supplied" to protect the identity of the source. At ABC News, leaving off attribution altogether was explained as a design decision. For example, with a feature photo essay that Jane Cowan produced, a single column with more white space on the sides and images integrated throughout the text and screen meant that captions and photo credits were eliminated. Usually, in such cases, photo credits are listed at the end of the story page, although this does not always eventuate. The practice of leaving off attribution in order to mask the unreliability of amateur sources (noted, for example, by Mast & Hanegreefs, 2015, p. 603) or to avoid potential negative evaluation of citizen imagery, as pointed out by Buehner Mortensen and Keshelashvili (2013), was not observed in this research project, neither through the interviews nor in the attribution practices around the use of citizen imagery in the empirical studies discussed in Chapters 3 and 4.

## Professional photography futures

All of the interviewees acknowledge the monumental disruptions of recent years that have seen staff photographers' transition out of a stable workplace and into the open/free market. They noted that options for photographers include becoming a freelancer and relying on their former employers to give them regular assignments, or becoming small business owners and taking on other photography work in the commercial/corporate sector or as wedding photographers to supplement their incomes (cf. Anderson & Young, 2016; Thomson, 2018). Some have thrived in this environment, while others have struggled with the need to promote themselves, to hunt down work, and to develop new contacts and relations. As Phil McLean explained, they are essentially small businesses and need all the marketing tricks they can muster. AAP has absorbed a number of photographers into their casual pool, and all other news organizations maintain their own lists of casuals that at the moment appear to be getting regular work. Stuart Watt describes the situation as a "classic case of disruption" and suggests that while younger people might adjust well to these sorts of working conditions, older generations with old-fashioned skill sets will find this transition very painful.

One of the risks with the outsourcing of this highly skilled work, in terms of both a technical and a news sense, as well as in relation to the physicality of the job (coping with the media scrum, being able to run backwards while still shooting reliable frames), is the loss of depth of experience that can be passed on to the next generation of photographers through workplace mentoring (see Thomson, 2018). Press photographers need to live through these experiences in order to learn from them. Phil McLean also suggested that photographers need to be specialists in order to make a good living. They need to dive deep into expertise. McLean went on to concede, however, that with such skills loss, Australia may need to look to other countries, with deeper reservoirs of skilled professionals, to start reinstating such experience and specialist knowledge. However, another way of combating the loss of skills, mentorship, and community was suggested by both McLean and King. AAP acknowledges the need to improve workplace culture for this increasingly casualized workforce and is attempting to build an inclusive workplace, organizing events to build community and to give people the space to talk through their workplace issues. At Fairfax Media, casuals are the first to engage with any professional development and training offered by King and her photojournalism colleagues. King is also very personally invested in the health and wellbeing of her photographers, treating them very much like a family.

One of the biggest hopes for the future, acknowledged by all interviewees, is the continuing value of the well-crafted photograph. As King states, "Photography adds value. It is the very thing that pulls the reader into a story". Watt adds, "Visual storytelling is a growth area, [and] highly produced work will become more visually sumptuous". It is just unclear who will provide the raw materials and under what circumstances they will be employed to do this. At News Corp Australia, Neil Bennett is very optimistic and sees the picture desk playing a central role in co-ordinating how images are sourced and processed. He states that everyone needs to adapt and recalibrate how we think about photography and where it comes from. He sees multiple layers of visual storytelling contributing to news reporting and new methods that take full advantage of the technical advances in the modern media company. He also sees the value in segmentation of the industry into specialist areas, which allows him to harness highly specialized and skilled freelance photography (e.g. for images of portraiture, sport, fashion, and investigative hard news stories).

On a personal note, one of the most rewarding (yet equally frustrating) aspects of this research project has been to hear Carly Earl express her ideas on the value of the professionally produced press photograph, specifically for the way in which it resonates with the words with which I have opened this book. She states that the professional photographer has the "ability to walk into a space and see something that nobody else does. Photography is a creative platform. It makes you feel stuff. The reason why you feel the way you do is because of them". The professional photographer can "get emotion out of an event that no-one else can . . . the one shot that can make you feel something".

On the flip side of such sentiment, however, is the fact that news organizations have been abandoning their photographers, and unless sentiments such as these are backed up by a willingness to fully remunerate professional photographers for their work, it is perhaps unlikely that such poignant moments captured from an event will be available for much longer. In the final chapter, I explore the effects of the disruptions to the Australian news media industry in relation to the findings presented in the last three chapters.

# 6 Professionals and amateurs
## Are we all in this together?

The remit of this book has been to investigate the effects of recent disruptions in the news media industry in Australia on the provision of visual news storytelling by major news media outlets. This final chapter reflects on the findings of both the empirical case studies and survey of routine reporting and the interviews conducted with industry professionals in relation to these disruptions. Where appropriate, these findings are discussed in relation to other research investigating similar disruptions in other news media markets.

## Australian photojournalism disrupted

In the Australian news media context, the facts of the disruptions to employment models are not in dispute. It is clear that employment models for photojournalists in Australia have been disrupted. The photography departments at both of the legacy news organizations, Fairfax Media and News Corp Australia, have been decimated. As the interviews in Chapter 5 revealed, Fairfax Media now works with nine staff photographers (it is uncertain whether these positions will be affected by the takeover by Nine Entertainment) servicing both the *Sydney Morning Herald* and sister national publication the *Australian Financial Review*. News Corp Australia works with a core staff of between 10 to 20 photographers and photo-editors across all of its metropolitan and regional newspapers. Both of these news organizations now work with lean photography departments, employing a very small core of salaried photographers providing exclusive photography to the mastheads first and foremost, as well as for subscription-based web stories. Much of the specialist (e.g. sport) and some daily diaried work have been outsourced to the news agency AAP, including the provision of photography to the regions and to community newspapers. Complementing this core of salaried positions is a vast network of freelance photographers, many of whom were formerly staff employed at these news organizations. The conditions in which freelance photographers are expected to work in this new environment are discussed in more detail in the next section.

What is in dispute in this volume is the effect of these disruptions, both on the sourcing of news photography and on the kinds of visual news storytelling that Australian news outlets are able to tell. I will address each of these issues in turn. Researchers have long lamented the loss of staff-employed professional news photographers, and some have indicated where the shortfall in the supply of news photography might come from. Láb and Štefaniková (2017, p. 18) for example use participant interviews with photojournalists and photo-editors in central Europe (Czech Republic, Poland, and Slovakia) to estimate that as much as 50 per cent of visual material published comes from a mix of "news agencies, image banks and freelancers". Gynnild (2017, p. 25) notes more generally that "news agency networks have become main suppliers of visual content to the news media". Through newsroom observations and interviews at a Swedish newspaper, Nilsson (2017, p. 47) notes an increased reliance on stock photos and archival images. In a study of a Flemish newspaper, de Smaele et al. (2017, p. 62) describe the visual decision making process of photo-editors as a process that is limited to "illustrating" the news, wherein the photo editor has three options for sourcing images to "match" a story: From a pool of freelance photographers, from among the images supplied by news agencies, or from an archive search.

These studies paint a valuable picture of the current state of affairs in relation to how visuals are sourced principally among European news organizations. However, without access to comparative studies on the sourcing of visuals at times when these news organizations were fully staffed with press photographers, it is difficult to assess the extent to which these sourcing practices are a significant shift away from previous practice. This is the same issue I face with the studies reported on in this volume. There are no comparative studies of how Australian news organizations sourced their photographs at times when newsrooms were fully staffed with press photographers. Thus, it is difficult to state categorically that sourcing practices have been disrupted and that news outlets now publish significantly more photographs supplied by news agencies or from other non-journalistic sources.

In relation to the sourcing of visuals from news agencies, image banks, and freelancers, the overall picture in Australia, in relation to routine, everyday news reporting practices is as follows: During the period surveyed for this volume, 32 per cent of news photographs were supplied by news agencies, 7 per cent came from freelance photographers, and 6 per cent of images were sourced from image banks, giving a total of 45 per cent of imagery being supplied in this way.[1] There are, however, significant differences between each of the news organizations in relation to these sources, which reflect the staffing models at each news organization. All four news organizations are enthusiastic users of agency photography. However, ABC News hardly ever makes use of freelance photographers (less than 1 per cent), whereas Fairfax Media and Guardian Australia frequently draw on freelancers (both at 16 per cent) for visual news coverage. As noted in Chapters 3 and 4, ABC News keeps much of its news production in-house, relying on a range of news workers to supply imagery for publication with news stories. This means there may be little need for freelancers (but see Stuart Watt, Chapter 5, on when and how ABC News does employ them). Guardian Australia, on the other hand, employs only one photographer and one picture editor/photographer, and with its Australian reporting covering every state and territory, it is inevitable that both agency and freelance photographers will be called upon to supply the majority of this coverage.

Another unique feature of the Australian news media market is the fact that the major supplier of agency news photography and copy, AAP, is co-owned by Fairfax Media and News Corp Australia. Thus, since the creation of this agency in 1935 (under the mandate of sharing the high expense of bringing international news into the country for the metropolitan newspapers, AAP, 2018), business models have been in place that cement a continuous supply of photography (and copy) to all of the Australian mastheads. Therefore, it is difficult to say with certainty that there have been significant changes in the amount of photography that is sourced via this news agency. The interviews do suggest that the supply of some diaried work has been handed over to AAP, but the extent to which this impacts on overall supply is difficult to estimate without comparative historical empirical data.[2]

In the studies reported in this volume, the use of image banks and stock imagery conformed largely to common practice around such imagery. As

---

1  The same overall figures in relation to the specialist case studies reported on in Chapter 3 are as follows: 13 per cent from agencies, 8 per cent from freelancers, and 0.3 per cent from image banks, giving a total of 21.3 per cent from such sources. This gives an average of 33 per cent of all imagery published by these news organizations being sourced from wire services, freelancers, and image banks.

2  The fact that the provision of community and regional news photography (at Fairfax Media and News Corp Australia) has been largely outsourced to AAP does not impact on the studies undertaken here. This is because the supply line for the publications I investigated comes first from the salaried photographers at the mastheads (as noted in the interviews in Chapter 5).

noted in Chapter 4, the stories that made use of stock images were about the economy, education, science and technology, and health, and largely concerned policy decisions or research findings rather than hard news events, thus conforming to the more conventional or clichéd uses of stock imagery. The use of stock photography to illustrate hard news reporting is still very rare in the Australian news media context. However, this is a potential sourcing practice that deserves closer and longer term investigation over the coming years.

Turning now to the effects of the disruptions to the Australian news media on the kinds of stories that these news organizations are able to tell, a much more complex picture emerges, particularly in relation to images sourced from amateurs/citizens and from social media. Amateur images have gained traction in academic research in recent years and are said to challenge journalists' thinking about what journalism is and what it should do (Andén-Papadopoulos & Pantti, 2013, p. 961; Allan, 2015, p. 467). Some researchers also question whether amateur visuals can be regarded as evidence of a democratization of the news-making process (Pantti & Bakker, 2009, p. 473). Much of this research has centred on the role of amateur images in the reporting of crisis events (see, for example, Andén-Papadopoulos & Pantti, 2014), and very little attention has been paid to how or if citizen images are taken up in routine news reporting.

In relation to crisis event reporting, Pantti (2013b) suggests that amateur images and video footage have the ability to affect how distant events are seen by politicians and audiences alike. Eyewitness images can be conceptualized as "voices demanding to be seen and heard", which "potentially enhance reporting by providing a wider variety of perspectives, by revealing new information and by effectively inviting us to feel responsible for the victims of the conflict through the raw aesthetics and involved perspective of the images presented" (Pantti, 2013b, p. 16). Amateur images may provide immediate updates on distant news events and bring news organizations and audiences closer to events (Pantti & Bakker, 2009, p. 475). They may also provide otherwise unobtainable evidence and even challenge professional journalism by "contradicting the mainstream news representations" (Pantti & Bakker, 2009, p. 475). More generally, Pantti (2013a) suggests that citizen images "are not only shaping news content, but also what is considered 'newsworthy'–which events become news and which are overlooked by the news media" (p. 203). If this is indeed the case, then the potential disruption to the kinds of visual news storytelling our news media are likely to engage in could be significant.

In the empirical studies reported on in this volume, an average of 8.5 per cent of images were sourced from named citizens and social media platforms (7 per cent in the specialist news reporting and 10 per cent in routine reporting).[3] As outlined in Chapters 3 and 4, the reasons for their use are complex. But to relate their use to the research discussed earlier, I would argue that only four stories were built around the existence of citizen imagery and concern events that might have been overlooked by the news media had such imagery not existed. These were two stories relating to the federal election in which the "bad behaviour" of politicians was captured on smartphones by members of the public (see Chapter 3). Both were published by Fairfax Media, and no other news organization reported on either of these events. Another two stories, published by News Corp Australia as part of their routine reporting, concern two road rage incidents in Sydney/New South Wales (discussed in detail in Chapter 4). Again, no other news organization reported on these incidents, and the verbal reporting in both cases foregrounds the existence of the footage. These stories appear to be written around the existence of the footage and could be considered examples of how the availability of visuals might "shape news content" in Pantti's (2013a) terms. However, if out of a total of 2,968 photographs examined in this research project, only 4 stories (making use of 14 images) were driven by the visuals that members of the public supplied, the extent of the influence of citizen imagery to drive and shape news content for the Australian news media might for now be considered minimal.

Research investigating the history of Australian press photography has been conducted by Anderson and Young (2016), and many of their conclusions are based on oral history interviews with 60 photographers. In their final chapter, they make the claim, "With the decline in staff photographers, newspapers not only use more stock photos, agency images, stills from TV, and social media images, they also use photographs supplied by the subjects of news" (Anderson & Young, 2016, p. 299). While they are absolutely correct in illustrating the wide range of sources that do supply imagery to the Australian news media (as corroborated by the empirical studies reported on in Chapters 3 and 4), I do contest the basis on which they suggest that there has been an increase in the use of some of these sources, for the reasons noted earlier (lack of comprehensive, empirical historical data). More importantly, I also contest the implication in their statement that the use of imagery supplied by story talent is a new phenomenon.

Newspapers have always drawn on a wide range of sources of photography in news reporting, including images supplied by the subjects of the news. As documented in Chapters 3 and 4, particularly in relation to hard news reporting where a person has died or is severely injured, the news

---

3 I talk about citizen and social media imagery together here because I found that almost all images sourced from social media were also taken by citizens.

media often publish portrait shots of the subject of the news, and such images can now readily be sourced from social media. What has been disrupted here is the way in which news organizations source such images, by searching public digital profiles of story subjects, most likely in the form of a social media account, rather than visiting the family home and requesting a copy of a photograph, as was common practice in the pre-digital era. Another common practice among newspapers is to use publicity shots (typically portraiture) supplied by story talent, particularly when they have been professionally produced. Again, the case studies in Chapter 3 illustrate this practice in relation to both the federal election and the Australian of the Year Awards, where professionally produced head shots supplied by candidates and award recipients were published. However, with no previous longitudinal empirical studies examining image-sourcing practices among Australian newspapers available for comparison, it is difficult to assess whether this represents a clear disruption of practices in the sourcing of photographs from the subject of the news.

Anderson and Young (2016, p. 299) illustrate their point regarding the use of photographs supplied by the subjects of news with an example about a "minor protest". They argue that the protest itself was not newsworthy enough to warrant coverage. However, since four poor-quality photographs were supplied by the protesters "the newspaper accepted them and made a prominent story out of them online" (p. 299). This is a very similar example to those given earlier, where the availability of visuals (regardless of their quality) may be perceived as compelling a news organization towards publication. However, it is important not to overstate the influence of such nonprofessionally sourced imagery on the kinds of news storytelling that the news media are able to tell. Stories built around the availability of imagery from citizens are still very rare and are sold to audiences as exactly that: Rare, unexpected, negative, and often norm breaking. This is certainly the case in relation to the road rage stories published by News Corp Australia in my dataset, where newsworthiness is discursively constructed through language choices such as "SHOCKING footage has emerged . . ." and "unleashed the perfect revenge . . . capturing the whole thing on a helmet cam" in relation to the obtained footage. Lexical choices such as "badly-behaved driver" and "a man punching a woman in the face during a violent incident" further emphasize the norm-breaking behaviour that has been exposed through this footage.

In summing up this section, I would contend that it is too early to tell whether there has been a major disruption to the sourcing of news photography in the Australian news media market. Further longitudinal studies are needed that monitor news publications for attribution practices around the news photography that does get published and comparisons made to the finding reported in this volume. News stories, particularly in the digital environment, are rarely published now without accompanying visuals, and these visuals have to be produced by someone or something (e.g. drones or robots). The Australian news media have always drawn on a wide range of sources in their news reporting, including citizens, and this has been demonstrated in the research reported in Chapters 3 and 4. Whether some sources are now more prevalent than in previous times is difficult to state with certainty.

I would also contend that there has not been a disruption to the *kinds* of visual news storytelling that the Australian news media are able to tell. This was particularly noticeable in the specialist case studies reported on in Chapter 3. Much of the photography, and with this the storytelling, conformed very much to expectations for each of those events. Citizens do feature among the sources drawn on for the supply of visuals in news storytelling, but again largely conform to tradition in how their images are used. While there was evidence in this research of a few stories (four) being created around the availability of citizen-produced imagery, I am reluctant to suggest that such use is shaping news content. Similar to Nilsson and Wadbring's (2015, p. 496) findings, there is also no evidence that amateurs are likely to push out professional photographers. The interviewees certainly acknowledged the distinct value of amateur imagery as well as its function in news storytelling, but none suggested that citizens compete with the work of professional photographers. Thus, to answer the question posed in the title of this chapter: In the case of the Australian news media, no, we are not all in this together. Yet.

Nevertheless, the interviewees in this research project believe that these are very exciting times for photography and that disruptions to the kinds of visual news storytelling that will be possible in the future have yet to be realized. Drones and virtual reality are two technologies that could have a huge impact on visual storytelling in journalism. However, it remains to be seen whether these technologies will suffer a similar fate as video has in the attempt to capture the hearts and minds of digitally engaged audiences (Banikarim, 2017; Moore, 2017; Hazard Owen, 2018).

Instead, I would contend that the major disruption to Australian photojournalism has come in the form of layoffs/redundancies. News organizations in Australia now have very limited staff resources for the supply of news photography, and it is inevitable that other sources are going to contribute more in the future. At the moment, former staff photographers who have now shifted over to the freelance market are taking on some of the shortfall in this supply, and it is in the transition to the freelance market that another major disruption has occurred, as will be discussed in the next section.

## You are now entering the precariat: proceed with caution

Over a four-year period between 2014 and 2017, the New Beats project surveyed more than 200 Australian journalists whose positions had been made redundant between 2012 to 2014. The aim of the project has been to "create greater understanding of the process and aftermath of redundancy in journalism and of the human effects and societal ramifications for an industry and occupation undergoing profound change" (Zion et al., 2018a, p. 5). Unfortunately, the report does not include responses from any of the photographers who were also made redundant during this period. However, the findings from this research do paint a very clear picture of the highs and lows of life after redundancy for Australian news media professionals. The New Beats project found that key challenges facing journalists post-redundancy include ageism (more than 50 per cent of respondents were over 50) and sexism, the fact that flexible work often means precarious income, and that professional identities were challenged (Zion et al., 2018b; see also Sherwood & O'Donnell, 2018 on professional identity). However, journalists were able to counterbalance the challenges of precarity by drawing on their skills and professionalism to take on new opportunities, often in unrelated forms of work (Zion et al., 2018b).

As the interviews in Chapter 5 suggest, for the photographers, this new-found precarity means working casual hours, often by the assignment, and with no guarantee of continued work. Being agile and flexible in how and when they work have become key skills for freelance photographers. Many also need to diversify, taking on photographic projects that may not have traditionally been part of their repertoires (e.g. corporate or wedding photography) since their labour in the news media market is insecure and unstable. This means also becoming much more aware of how to budget and to account for lean times when there is no work at all. As noted by the interviewees in Chapter 5, some have thrived in this environment, while others have struggled with the need to promote themselves, to hunt down work, and to develop new contacts and relations. The Australian news media market is very small, and while assisting photographers to transition to the freelance model, re-employing them on casual contracts, offering professional development, and allowing them to retain copyright of their work after publication may all seem like admirable attempts at acknowledging the value of their work, there are both worrying and somewhat contradictory implications emerging as a result of this particular disruption.

Journalism is built on the principle of serving the public interest. This means that, for most news workers, journalism is a life-defining job, and this is especially true for the photographers. They not only put their lives on the line, quite literally, when covering certain kinds of assignments or breaking news events, they also need tremendous creative capacity to find that defining moment in an event that has the potential to become the story and to change the way people operate in the world. This is the kind of photography that editors, including those interviewed for this research project, still crave (see Chapter 5). If a fully casualized workforce is the way forward for the Australian news media market, one that provides no safety net for news workers, then that passion for working in and for the public interest will dwindle. To put it in the words of Standing (2014) in relation to what he calls "a class-in-the-making" – the precariat: Under such a model, there is "no sense of loyalty or commitment in either direction. For the precariat, jobs are instrumental, not life defining. The alienation from labour is taken for granted" (Standing, 2014, p. 4). The key question is: Has the job of the press photographer become merely instrumental? If it has, then this probably represents the biggest disruption of all to visual news storytelling.

Ultimately, the future of press photography rests once again on the value placed in both the photographer and the photograph, and the willingness of those in positions of power to support and pay for them. As Thomson (2018, p. 816) notes, "By offering exposure rather than a sustainable wage, the freelancer model devalues a photographer's work and forces them to be innovative and entrepreneurial in order to survive". But for many, mere survival is simply unacceptable.

To conclude, this book-length treatment of the disruptions to photojournalism stands as a benchmark for the current state of affairs for news photography in Australia. To complement insights gained from the intuitions, memories, and statements of professionals, this mixed-methods, interdisciplinary project has incorporated empirically grounded investigations of news photography. In so doing, it has offered a clear picture of sourcing and attribution practices, both in relation to specialist reporting and in relation to everyday, routine reporting. Its empirical base allows for future replication and the ability to reliably track actual shifts and disruptions in how visual news reporting in Australia will evolve over the coming decades.

# Appendix

Table A1 Inventory of visual devices that often construct newsworthiness in English-language news

| News value | Visual devices |
|---|---|
| *Aesthetic Appeal* (the event is discursively constructed as beautiful) | **Content:** **Represented participants:** • The depiction of people, places, objects, landscapes culturally recognized for their beauty **Capture:** **Composition: Balance** • Dynamic, asymmetric composition, making use of diagonal axis • Balanced, symmetrical images where the symmetry is momentarily interrupted **Technical affordances:** • Movement: Blurring and freezing of action • Noise: High level of graininess • Focus: Lengthening or reducing depth of field within the image |
| *Consonance* (the event is discursively constructed as [stereo]typical) | **Content:** **Represented participants/attributes:** • The depiction of people and their attributes that fit with the stereotypical imagery of a person/country, etc. (e.g. beer and breasts for Germany's Oktoberfest) **Activity sequence:** • Staged/highly choreographed depictions of typical activities associated with a person/group/nation |

| | |
|---|---|
| *Eliteness*<br>(the event is discursively constructed as of high status or fame) | **Content:**<br>**Represented participants:**<br>• Showing known and easily recognizable key figures, e.g. political leaders, celebrities<br>**Attributes:**<br>• Showing people in elaborate costumes, uniforms, or with other regalia of officialdom<br>• Showing self-reflexive elements like microphones/cameras<br>**Activity sequence:**<br>• Showing people flanked by military, police or bodyguards, or in a media scrum<br>• Showing people using the specialist equipment associated with elite professions (e.g. surgeon performing an operation)<br>**Setting:**<br>• Showing context associated with an elite profession, e.g. books, lab, police station |
| *Impact*<br>(the event is discursively constructed as having significant effects or consequences) | **Content:**<br>**Represented participants/attributes:**<br>• Showing the after-effects (often negative) of events, e.g. scenes of destruction, injuries, damage to property<br>• Showing emotions caused by an event |
| *Negativity*<br>(the event is discursively constructed as negative) | **Content:**<br>**Represented participants/attributes:**<br>• Showing negative events and their effects, e.g. the aftermath of accidents, natural disasters, the injured/wounded, the wreckage/damage done to property<br>• Showing people experiencing negative emotions<br>**Activity sequence:**<br>• Showing people being arrested or (as defendant) with lawyers/barristers/police<br>• Showing people attempting to hide their identities, e.g. using an item of clothing to cover the head or showing aggression towards the camera, e.g. putting a hand up in front of the lens<br>• Showing people engaging in norm-breaking behaviour, e.g. fighting, vandalizing, stealing, attacking |

*(Continued)*

Table A1 (Continued)

| News value | Visual devices |
|---|---|
| | **Capture:**<br>**Technical affordances:**<br>• Movement/blurring involving negative content, resulting in poor-quality images<br>• Noise: Dramatizing and intensifying negative content<br>• Focus: Where extreme circumstances mean unable to provide sharp and detailed image content, e.g. water/rain on the lens<br>• In moving images: Blurring and movement caused by camera-people moving around, running, ducking to avoid projectiles, etc. (suggesting unstable situation, i.e. danger) |
| *Positivity*<br>(the event is discursively constructed as positive) | **Content:**<br>**Represented participants/attributes:**<br>• Showing people experiencing positive emotions<br>**Activity sequence:**<br>• Showing people engaging in positively valued behaviour, e.g. being successful at red carpet events, award ceremonies<br>• Showing actions associated with reconciliation or praise, e.g. shaking hands, hugging |
| *Personalisation*<br>(the event is discursively constructed as having a personal/human face) | **Content:**<br>**Represented participants/attributes:**<br>• Showing "ordinary" individuals, especially when singled out and standing in for a larger group<br>• People dressed in informal/everyday clothing<br>• Carrying items such as rucksacks, handbags, shopping bags<br>• Showing an emotional response<br>**Setting:**<br>• In the home/domestic setting<br>• On the street |

| | Capture: |
|---|---|
| | **Composition: Salience** |
| | • Positioning individuals in unequal relation (in terms of textual composition, NOT in terms of social power dynamics) to others in the image frame, e.g. singling out one individual through foregrounding or backgrounding |
| | **Composition: Shot length** |
| | • Using a close-up shot (to focus on a person's emotion, for example) |
| | **Technical affordances: Focus** |
| | • Reducing depth of field so that the focus remains on the individual |
| *Proximity* | **Content:** |
| (the event is discursively constructed as geographically or culturally near) | **Represented participants/attributes/setting:** |
| | • Showing well-known or iconic landmarks (Tower Bridge, Sydney Opera House, Golden Gate Bridge), natural features (Uluru), or cultural symbols (flags, national colours/distinctive uniforms) |
| | **[Verbal text:** |
| | • Showing verbal text indicating relevant place/cultural connection, e.g. signage] |
| *Superlativeness* | **Content:** |
| (the event is discursively constructed as being of high intensity/large scope) | **Represented participants:** |
| | • Showing the large-scale repetition of participants in the image frame, e.g. not just one house but an entire street affected |
| | • Showing extreme (positive or negative) emotions in participants |
| | **Capture:** |
| | **Composition: Shot length** |
| | • Use of very wide angle to exaggerate differences in size/space |
| | • Magnification (larger than life representation) through use of extreme close-up or macro lens |
| | **Technical affordances: Movement** |
| | • Camera movement and blurring, combined with camera people moving around, running, ducking to avoid projectiles, etc. (suggesting seriousness/high danger, etc) |

(*Continued*)

Table A1 (Continued)

| News value | Visual devices |
|---|---|
| *Timeliness* (the event is discursively constructed as recent, ongoing, about to happen, new, current, seasonal) | **Content:** **Represented participants:**<br>• Natural phenomena that indicate time, e.g. the season may be implied in flora or environmental conditions<br>• Inclusion of cultural artefacts, like Christmas trees that are representative of a particular time of year<br><br>**Activity sequence:**<br>• Showing the revealing of an item, to be seen for the first time<br><br>**[Verbal Text:**<br>• Including verbal text indicating relevant time, e.g. signage] |
| *Unexpectedness* (the event is discursively constructed as unexpected) | **Content:** **Represented participants:**<br>• Showing people being shocked/surprised<br>• Showing unusual happenings that would be considered outside an established societal norm or expectation<br><br>**Capture:** **Composition: Salience**<br>• Juxtaposition of elements in the frame that create stark contrast |

# References

AAP (2018). *Our History: Australian Associated Press.* Accessed 18 May 2018. www.AAP.com.au/our-history/

About Us (2019). Nine Entertainment. Accessed 10 January 2019. www.nineenter tainmentco.com.au/about-us

Allan, S. (2013). *Citizen Witnessing: Revisioning Journalism in Times of Crisis.* Cambridge: Polity Press.

Allan, S. (2015). Introduction: Photojournalism and citizen journalism. *Journalism Practice*, 9(4), 455–464.

Allan, S. & Peters, C. (2015). Visual truths of citizen reportage: Four research problematics. *Information, Communication & Society*, 18(11), 1348–1361.

Andén-Papadopoulos, K. & Pantti, M. (2013). Re-imagining crisis reporting: Professional ideology of journalists and citizen eyewitness images. *Journalism: Theory, Practice and Criticism*, 14(7), 960–977.

Andén-Papadopoulos, K. & Pantti, M. (Eds.) (2014). *Amateur Images and Global News.* Bristol: Intellect.

Anderson, C.W., Bell, E.J. & Shirky, C. (2014). *Post Industrial Journalism: Adapting to the Present.* New York: Columbia University Academic Commons. https://doi.org/10.7916/D8N01JS7

Anderson, F. (2014). Chasing the pictures: Press and magazine photography. *Media International Australia*, 150, 47–55.

Anderson, M. (2013). At newspapers, photographers feel the brunt of job cuts. *Pew Research Centre*, 11 November. Accessed 12 January 2015. www.pewresearch.org/fact-tank/2013/11/11/at-newspapers-photographers-feel-the-brunt-of-job-cuts/

Anderson, F. & Young, S. (2016). *Shooting the Picture: Press Photography in Australia.* Melbourne: The Miegunyah Press.

*Australia Day Council* (2018). About Australia day. Accessed 17 January 2019. www.australiaday.org.au/about-australia-day/

Banikarim, S. (2017). R.I.P. Pivot to Video (2017–2017). *NiemanLab*, 31 December. Accessed 25 January 2019. www.niemanlab.org/2017/12/r-i-p-pivot-to-video-2017-2017/

Becker, K. (2013). Performing the news. *Photographies*, 6(1), 17–28.

Becker, K. (2015). Gestures of seeing: Amateur photographers in the news. *Journalism*, 16(4), 451–469.

Becker, K.E. (1992). Photojournalism and the tabloid press. In P. Dahlgren & C. Sparks (Eds.), *Journalism and Popular Culture* (pp. 130–153). London: Sage.

Bednarek, M. & Caple, H. (2017). *The Discourse of News Values: How News Organizations Create Newsworthiness*. New York: Oxford University Press.

Benton, J. (2012). Clay Christensen on the news industry: "We didn't quite understand . . . how quickly things fall off the cliff". *Neiman Journalism Lab*, 18 October. Accessed 18 April 2018. www.niemanlab.org/2012/10/clay-christensen-on-the-news-industry-we-didnt-quite-understand-how-quickly-things-fall-off-the-cliff/

Blocker, J. (2009). *Seeing Witness: Visuality and the Ethics of Testimony*. Minneapolis/London: University of Minnesota Press.

Bodey, M. & Ackerman, P. (2014). Staff in 'unlawful' walkout as Fairfax swings the jobs axe again. *Australian*, 8 May. Accessed 22 January 2019. www.abc.net.au/mediawatch/transcripts/1514_oz.pdf

Bowers, M. (2014). Photography requires skill. It's sad to see good Fairfax employees being let go. *Guardian Australia*, 7 May. Accessed 12 March 2016. www.theguardian.com/commentisfree/2014/may/07/photography-requires-skills-its-sad-to-see-fairfax-let-good-employees-go

Brennen, B. (1998). Strategic Competition and the value of photographers' work: Photojournalism in Gannett Newspapers, 1937–1947. *American Journalism*, 15(2), 59–77.

Bruns, A. (2017). The ABC is not siphoning audiences from Fairfax. *The Conversation*, 26 May. Accessed 29 May 2017. https://theconversation.com/the-abc-is-not-siphoning-audiences-from-fairfax-78329

Buehner Mortensen, T. & Keshelashvili, A. (2013). If everyone with a camera can do this, then what? Professional photojournalists' sense of professional threat in the face of citizen photojournalism. *Visual Communication Quarterly*, 20(3), 144–158.

Campbell, D. (2013). *Visual Storytelling in the Age of Post-Industrialist Journalism*. Amsterdam: World Press Photo.

Caple, H. (2010). What you see and what you get: The evolving role of news photographs in an Australian broadsheet. In V. Rupar (Ed.), *Journalism and Meaning-Making: Reading the Newspaper* (pp. 199–220). Cresskill, NJ: Hampton Press.

Caple, H. (2013). *Photojournalism: A Social Semiotic Approach*. Basingstoke: Palgrave Macmillan.

Caple, H. (2018a). News values and newsworthiness. In *Oxford Research Encyclopedia of Communication*. Oxford: Oxford University Press.

Caple, H. (2018b). Lucy says today she is a Labordoodle: How the dogs-of-Instagram reveal voter preferences. *Social Semiotics*. [Ahead-of-print] DOI: 10.1080/10350330.2018.1443582

Caple, H. (2019). Image-centric practices on Instagram: Subtle shifts in footing. In H. Stöckl, H. Caple & J. Pflaeging (Eds.), *Image-Centric Practices in the Contemporary Media Sphere* (n.p.). London/New York: Routledge.

Caple, H. & Dunn, A. (2009). Educating aunty: How prepared are ABC entry-level journalists for the digital age? In T. Cullen (Ed.), *Journalism Education in the*

*Digital Age: Sharing Strategies and Experiences* (n.p.). Perth, WA: Journalism Education Association of Australia Conference.

Caple, H., Huan, C. & Bednarek, M. (in preparation) *The Newsworthiness of National Holidays: A Cross-cultural Discursive News Values Analysis of the Chinese National Day and Australia Day*.

Caple, H. & Knox, J.S. (2012). Online news galleries, photojournalism and the photo essay. *Visual Communication*, 11(2), 207–236.

Caple, H. & Knox, J.S. (2015). A framework for the multimodal analysis of online news galleries. *Social Semiotics*, 25(3), 292–321.

Caple, H. & Knox, J.S. (2017). How to author a picture gallery. *Journalism: Theory, Practice and Criticism*. [Ahead-of-print] DOI: https://doi.org/10.1177/1464884917691988

Channick, R. (2013). Chicago Sun-Times lays off its photo staff. *Chicago Tribune*, 30 May. Accessed 25 January 2019. www.chicagotribune.com/business/ct-xpm-2013-05-30-chi-chicago-sun-times-photo-20130530-story.html

Chouliaraki, L. & Blaagaard, B. (2013). Special issue: The ethics of images. *Visual Communication*, 12(3), 253–259.

Creswell, J.W. (2003). *Research Design: Qualitative, Quantitative, and Mixed Methods Approaches*, 2nd edition. Thousand Oaks, CA: Sage.

Davidson, H. (2016). Election result 'Muddle' is Turnbull's Fault, says NT Labor MP Warren Snowdon. *Guardian Australia*, 3 July. Accessed 6 April 2017. www.theguardian.com/australianews/2016/jul/04/election-result-muddle-turnbulls-fault-nt-labor-mp-warren-snowdon

de Smaele, H., Geenen, E. & De Cock, R. (2017). Visual gatekeeping – Selection of news photographs at a Flemish newspaper. A qualitative inquiry into the photo news desk. *Nordicom Review*, 38(2), 57–70.

Deuze, M. (2006). Participation, remediation, bricolage: Considering principal components of a digital culture. *The Information Society*, 22, 63–75.

Dwyer, T. (2016). FactCheck: Is Australia's level of media ownership concentration one of the highest in the world? *The Conversation*, 12 December. Accessed 18 February 2018. https://theconversation.com/factcheck-is-australias-level-of-media-ownership-concentration-one-of-the-highest-in-the-world-68437

Edley, N. & Litosseliti, L. (2010). Contemplating interviews and focus groups. In L. Litosseliti (Ed.), *Research Methods in Linguistics* (pp. 155–179). London: Continuum.

Estrin, J. (2017). The uncertain future of photojournalism. *The New York Times, Lens*, 15 February. Accessed 19 February 2018. https://lens.blogs.nytimes.com/2017/02/15/the-uncertain-future-of-photojournalism/

Evans, K. (2001). *Still: A Cultural History of Press Photography in Australia*. PhD Thesis. Sydney: University of Technology Sydney.

Feez, S., Iedema, R. & White, P.R.R. (2008). *Media Literacy*. Surry Hills, NSW: NSW Adult Migrant Education Service.

Feik, N. (2017). Killing our media: The impact of Facebook and the tech giants. *The Monthly*, July, pp. 24–33.

Franklin, B. (2018). *Disruptions: Studies in Digital Journalism* [Flyer].

Fuller, G. (2014). Journalism jobs. *Event Mechanics*, 2 June. Accessed 9 January 2019. http://eventmechanics.net.au/2014/06/journalism-jobs/

Greenwood, K. & Thomas, R.J. (2015). Locating the journalism in citizen photojournalism: The use and content of citizen-generated imagery. *Digital Journalism*, 3(4), 615–633.

Greenslade, R. (2012). Why newspapers are closing the shutters on staff photographers. *The Guardian, Media*, 24 January. Accessed 19 February 2018. www.the guardian.com/media/greenslade/2012/jan/24/news-photography-theindependent

Greenslade, R. (2016). Almost 60% of US newspaper jobs vanish in 26 years. *The Guardian, Media*, 6 June. Accessed 16 August 2018. www.theguardian.com/media/greenslade/2016/jun/06/almost-60-of-us-newspaper-jobs-vanish-in-26-years

Grigg, A. (2018). Greg Hywood announces his own redundancy, $8.2m pay day. *Australian Financial Review*, 27 July. Accessed 10 January 2019. www.afr.com/business/media-and-marketing/publishing/greg-hywood-likely-to-receive-82-million-from-fairfax-takeover-20180726-h136vb

Gynnild, A. (2017). The visual power of news agencies. *Nordicom Review*, 38(2), 25–39.

Hadland, A., Lambert, P. & Barnett, C. (2016). *The State of News Photography 2016: A Survey of Photojournalists' Attitudes Toward Work Practices, Technology and Life in the Digital Age*. Amsterdam: World Press Photo/University of Stirling.

Hare, K. & LaForme, R. (2018). These tools will help you find the right images for your stories. *Poynter, Innovation*, 8 February. Accessed 20 February 2018. www.poynter.org/news/these-tools-will-help-you-find-right-images-your-stories

Harkin, J., Anderson, K., Morgan, L. & Smith, B. (2012). *Deciphering User-Generated Content in Transitional Societies: A Syria Coverage Case Study*. Philadelphia: Center for Global Communication Studies, Annenberg School for Communication, University of Pennsylvania.

Hazard Owen, L. (2018). Did Facebook's faulty data push news publishers to make terrible decisions on video? *NiemanLab*, 17 October. Accessed 25 January 2019. www.niemanlab.org/2018/10/did-facebooks-faulty-data-push-news-publishers-to-make-terrible-decisions-on-video/

Heilpern, W. (2016). Briefing: How 'deceptive' sponsored news articles could be tricking readers – even with a disclosure message. *Business Insider Australia*, 18 March. Accessed 31 July 2017. www.businessinsider.com/how-deceptive-sponsored-news-articles-could-be-undermining-trusted-news-brands-even-with-a-disclosure-message-2016–3#krieXrCGCZ0hif6y.99

Hermida, A. & Thurman, N. (2008). A clash of cultures: The integration of user-generated content within professional journalistic frameworks at British newspaper websites. *Journalism Practice*, 2(3), 343–356.

Hester, J.B. & Dougall, E. (2007). The efficiency of constructed week sampling for content analysis of online news. *Journalism & Mass Communication Quarterly*, 84(4), 811–824.

Hoskins, A. & O'Loughlin, B. (2010). *War and Media: The Emergence of Diffused War*. Cambridge: Polity Press.

IBIS World (2017). *Newspaper Publishing – Australia Market Research Report*, June 2017. Accessed 16 August 2018. www.ibisworld.com.au/industry-trends/

market-research-reports/information-media-telecommunications/except-internet-music-publishing/newspaper-publishing.html

IBIS World (2018). *Newspaper Publishing – Australia Market Research Report*, June 2018. Accessed 10 January 2019. www.ibisworld.com.au/industry-trends/market-research-reports/information-media-telecommunications/except-internet-music-publishing/newspaper-publishing.html

Johnson, R.B., Onwuegbuzie, A.J. & Turner, L.A. (2007). Toward a definition of mixed methods research. *Journal of Mixed Methods Research*, 1(2), 112–133.

Kakar, A. (2018). Some 40 UK local newspapers closed in 2017 with net loss of 45 jobs, new research shows. *Press Gazette*, 27 March. Accessed 16 August 2018. www.pressgazette.co.uk/some-40-uk-local-newspapers-closed-in-2017-with-net-loss-of-45-jobs-new-research-shows/

Karp, P. (2016). Election shows majority support same-sex marriage, LGBTI groups claim. *Guardian Australia*, 3 July. Accessed 6 April 2017. www.theguardian.com/australia-news/2016/jul/03/election-shows-majority-support-same-sex-marriage-lgbti-groups-claim

Kelly, V. (2018). AAP to cut up to 25 positions as demand for services reduces. *Mumbrella*, 5 June. Accessed 28 November 2018. https://mumbrella.com.au/AAP-to-cut-up-to-25-positions-as-demand-for-services-reduces-521922

Kidd, J. (2014a). ABC cuts: Staff told 100 jobs to go from news division. ABC News, 24 November. Accessed 28 November 2018. www.abc.net.au/news/2014-11-24/abc-news-division-to-lose-100-staff/5913668

Kidd, J. (2014b). ABC cuts: Managing director Mark Scott announces more than 400 jobs to go. ABC News, 25 November. Accessed 28 November 2018. www.abc.net.au/news/2014-11-24/mark-scott-announces-abc-job-cuts/5913082

Knox, J.S. (2019). Multimodal mobile news: Design and images in tablet-platform apps. In H. Stöckl, H. Caple & J. Pflaeging (Eds.), *Image-Centric Practices in the Contemporary Media Sphere* (n.p.). London/New York: Routledge.

Kress, G. & van Leeuwen, T.J. (2006). *Reading Images The Grammar of Visual Design*, 2nd edition. London/New York: Routledge.

Láb, F. & Štefaniková, S. (2017). Photojournalism in central Europe: Editorial and working practices. *Nordicom Review*, 38(2), 7–23.

Lacy, S., Riffe, D., Stoddard, S., Martin, H. & Chang, K. (2001). Sample size for newspaper content analysis in multiyear studies. *Journalism & Mass Communication Quarterly*, 78, 836–845.

Lang, B. (2011). CNN lays off 50 staffers after employee appreciation week. *Reuters*, 11 November. Accessed 29 May 2017. www.reuters.com/article/2011/11/11/idUS39879393020111111

Lee, J. (2012). News plans to shed photographers. *Sydney Morning Herald*, 16 August. Accessed 24 August 2017. www.smh.com.au/business/media-and-marketing/news-plans-to-shed-photographers-20120816-24apv.html

Leslie, T. (2016). What. Just. Happened? ABC News, 5 July. Accessed 6 April 2017. www.abc.net.au/news/2016-07-03/election-results-what-just-happened/7553916

Luke, D.A., Caburnay, A. & Cohen, E.L. (2011). How much is enough? New recommendations for using constructed week sampling in newspaper content analysis of health stories. *Communication Methods and Measures*, 5(1), 76–91.

Machin, D. & Niblock, S. (2008). Branding newspapers. *Journalism Studies*, 9(2), 244–259.

Machin, D. & van Leeuwen, T.J. (2007). *Global Media Discourse*. London/New York: Routledge.

Macnamara, J. (2012). As the 'rivers of gold' dry up, what business model will save media? *The Conversation*, 29 June. Accessed 12 January 2015. http://theconversation.com/as-the-rivers-of-gold-dry-up-what-business-model-will-save-media-7956

Mast, J. & Hanegreefs, S. (2015). When news media turn to citizen-generated images of war: Transparency and graphicness in the visual coverage of the Syrian conflict. *Digital Journalism*, 3(4), 594–614.

MEAA (2018). *Media, Entertainment and Arts Alliance* (MEAA). Submission to the Australian Competition and Consumer Commission's Digital Platforms Inquiry, April.

Meade, A. (2014). News Corp Australia leaked accounts show 1,000 jobs cut across mastheads. *Guardian Australia*, 20 August. Accessed 24 August 2017. www.theguardian.com/media/2014/aug/20/news-corp-australia-leaked-accounts-show-1000-jobs-cut-across-mastheads

Meade, A. (2018a). ABC axes another 37 jobs in wake of $84m budget cut. *Guardian Australia*, 1 June. Accessed 28 November 2018. www.theguardian.com/media/2018/jun/01/abc-axes-another-37-jobs-in-wake-of-84m-budget-cut

Meade, A. (2018b). Almost 150 jobs to go as Fairfax and nine merger restructure revealed. *Guardian Australia*, 3 December. Accessed 9 January 2019. www.theguardian.com/media/2018/dec/03/almost-150-jobs-to-go-as-fairfax-and-nine-merger-restructure-revealed

Moore, H.M. (2017). The secret cost of pivoting to video. *Columbia Journalism Review*, 26 September. Accessed 25 January 2019. www.cjr.org/business_of_news/pivot-to-video.php

Murphy, K. & Karp, P. (2016). Malcolm Turnbull cannot command his party and should resign, Bill Shorten says. *Guardian Australia*, 4 July. Accessed 6 April 2017. www.theguardian.com/australia-news/2016/jul/04/malcolm-turnbull-cannot-command-his-party-and-shouldresign-bill-shorten-says

New Beats (2017). Submission to the select committee on the future of public interest journalism. Submission 37.

Newman, N., Fletcher, R., Kalogeropoulos, A., Levy, D.A.L. & Kleis Nielsen, R. (2017). *Reuters Institute Digital News Report 2017*. Oxford: RISJ.

Nilsson, M. (2017). A faster kind of photojournalism: Image-selection processes in a Swedish newsroom. *Nordicom Review*, 38(2), 41–56.

Nilsson, M. & Wadbring, I. (2015). Not good enough? Amateur images in the regular news flow of print and online newspapers. *Journalism Practice*, 9(4), 484–501.

O'Donnell, P., Zion, L. & Sherwood, M. (2016). Where do journalists go after newsroom job cuts? *Journalism Practice*, 10(1), 35–51.

Pantti, M. (2013a). Getting closer? Encounters of the national media with global images. *Journalism Studies*, 14(2), 201–218.

Pantti, M. (2013b). Seeing and not seeing the Syrian crisis: New visibility and the visual framing of the Syrian conflict in seven newspapers and their online editions. *JOMEC Journal*, 4, 1–22.

Pantti, M. & Andén-Papadopoulos, K. (2011). Transparency and trustworthiness: Strategies for incorporating amateur photography into news discourse. In K. Andén-Papadopoulos & M. Pantti (Eds.), *Amateur Images and Global News* (pp. 97–112). Bristol: Intellect.

Pantti, M. & Bakker, P. (2009). Misfortunes, memories and sunsets: Non-professional images in Dutch news media. *International Journal of Cultural Studies*, 12(5), 471–489.

Pope, K. (2018). So you wanna be a journalist? *Columbia Journalism Review*, Spring/Summer. Accessed 8 June 2018. www.cjr.org/special_report/journalism-jobs.php/

Reich, Z. & Klein-Avraham, I. (2014). Textual DNA: The hindered authorship of photojournalists in the Western press. *Journalism Practice*, 8(5), 619–631.

Riffe, D., Aust, C.F. & Lacy, S.R. (1993). The effectiveness of random, consecutive day and constructed week sampling in newspaper content analysis. *Journalism Quarterly*, 70, 133–139.

Robertson, J. & Meade, A. (2017). Fairfax boss Greg Hywood was paid as much as $7.2m in 2016. *Guardian Australia*, 8 May. Accessed 29 May 2017. www.the guardian.com/media/2017/may/09/fairfax-boss-greg-hywood-paid-more-2016

Robin, M. (2016). More BBC on the ABC: Full news division cuts revealed. *Crikey, Media Briefs*, 18 May. Accessed 29 May 2017. www.crikey.com.au/2016/05/18/more-bbc-on-the-abc-full-news-division-cuts-revealed/

Samios, Z. (2018a). ABC to axe 20 metro newsroom jobs as it restructures to adapt to 'modern media environment. *Mumbrella*, 30 April. Accessed 20 November 2018. https://mumbrella.com.au/abc-to-axe-20-metro-newsroom-jobs-as-it-restructures-to-adapt-to-modern-media-environment-514329

Samios, Z. (2018b). News Corp axes Adelaide photography, sub-editing and production roles. *Mumbrella*, 14 May. Accessed 20 November 2018. https://mumbrella.com.au/news-corp-axes-photography-sub-editing-and-production-roles-in-adelaide-517274

Sherwood, M. & O'Donnell, P. (2018). Once a journalist, always a journalist? *Journalism Studies*, 19(7), 1021–1038.

Simons, M. (2012). *Journalism at the Crossroads: Crisis and Opportunity for the Press*. Brunswick: Scribe.

Singer, J.B. (2005). The political J-blogger: 'Normalizing' a new media form to fit old norms and practices. *Journalism*, 6(2), 173–198.

Singer, J.B. (2011). Taking responsibility: Legal and ethical issues in participatory journalism. In J.B. Singer, D. Domingo, A. Heinonen, A. Hermida, S. Paulussen, T. Quandt, Z. Reich & M. Vujnovic (Eds.), *Participatory Journalism: Guarding Open Gates at Online Newspapers* (pp. 121–138). Chichester: Wiley-Blackwell.

Sjøvaag, H. (2011). Amateur images and journalistic authority. In K. Andén-Papadopoulos & M. Pantti (Eds.), *Amateur Images and Global News* (pp. 79–95). Bristol, UK: Intellect.

Skok, D. (2012). Finding a way forward. *Nieman Reports*, 6(3), 4–5.

Sontag, S. (2003). *Regarding the Pain of Others*. London: Hamish Hamilton.

Standing, G. (2014). The precariat and class struggle, "O precariado e a luta de classes", *Revista Crítica de Ciências Sociais*, 103, 9–24.

Starfield, S. (2010). Ethnographies. In B. Paltridge & A. Phakiti (Eds.), *Continuum Companion to Research Methods in Applied Linguistics* (pp. 50–65). London: Continuum.

Taubert, E. (2012). So, you're still using the phrase citizen-journalism? *Daily Crowdsource*. Accessed 12 January 2015. http://dailycrowdsource.com/content/crowdsourcing/1092-so-you-re-still-using-the-phrase-citizen-journalism

Taylor, L. (2018). ACCC will have power to grill Google and Facebook on threat to news media. *Guardian Australia*, 26 February. Accessed 17 January 2019. www.theguardian.com/media/2018/feb/26/accc-will-have-power-to-grill-google-and-facebook-on-threat-to-news-media?

Thompson, D. (2016). The print apocalypse and how to survive it. *The Atlantic*, 3 November. Accessed 19 February 2018. www.theatlantic.com/business/archive/2016/11/the-print-apocalypse-and-how-to-survive-it/506429/

Thomson, T.J. (2018). Freelance photojournalists and photo editors: Learning and adapting in a (mostly faceless) virtual world. *Journalism Studies*, 19(6), 803–823.

Usher, N. (2011). Professional journalists, hands off! Citizen journalism as civic responsibility. In R.W. McChesney & V. Pickard (Eds.), *Will the Last Reporter Please Turn Out the Lights: The Collapse of Journalism and What Can Be Done to Fix It* (pp. 264–276). New York: New Press.

Walkley Media Talks (2016). *Shots from the Front*. State Gallery of NSW: Walkley Foundation, 21 July.

Ward, M. (2017a). News Corp reveals drastic restructure including most photographers being made redundant. *Mumbrella*, 11 April. Accessed 20 November 2018. https://mumbrella.com.au/news-corp-cut-jobs-looks-streamline-editorial-operations-438319

Ward, M. (2017b). News Corp restructure moves ahead with photographer positions made redundant. *Mumbrella*, 16 May. Accessed 20 November 2018. https://mumbrella.com.au/news-corp-restructure-moves-ahead-photographer-positions-made-redundant-445037

Welling, W. (1987). *Photography in America: The Formative Years, 1839–1900*. Albuquerque: University of New Mexico Press.

Wojdynski, B.W. & Evans, N.J. (2016). Going native: Effects of disclosure position and language on the recognition and evaluation of online native advertising. *Journal of Advertising*, 45(2), 157–168.

Young, S. (2010). The journalism "crisis": Is Australia immune or just ahead of its time? *Journalism Studies*, 11(4), 610–624.

Young, S. & Carson, A. (2018). What is a journalist? The view from employers as revealed by their job vacancy advertisements. *Journalism Studies*, 19(3), 452–472.

Zelizer, B. (1998). *Remembering to Forget: Holocaust Memory Through the Camera's Eye*. Chicago/London: University of Chicago Press.

Zelizer, B. (2004). When war is reduced to a photograph. In S. Allan & B. Zelizer (Eds.), *Reporting War: Journalism in Wartime* (pp. 115–135). London/New York: Routledge.

Zelizer, B. (2005). Journalism through the camera's eye. In S. Allan (Ed.), *Journalism: Critical Issues* (pp. 167–176). Maidenhead: Open University Press.

Zion, L. (2013). New beats: Where do redundant journalists go? *The Conversation*, 2 December. Accessed 13 January 2015. https://theconversation.com/new-beats-where-do-redundant-journalists-go-20710

Zion, L., Dodd, A., Ricketson, M., Sherwood, M., Winarnita, M., O'Donnell, P. & Marjoribanks, T. (2018b). New research reveals how Australian journalists are faring four years after redundancy. *The Conversation*, 5 December. Accessed 10 January 2019. https://theconversation.com/new-research-reveals-how-australian-journalists-are-faring-four-years-after-redundancy-107520

Zion, L., Sherwood, M., O'Donnell, P., Marjoribanks, T., Ricketson, M., Dodd, A. & Winarnita, M. (2018a). *New Beats Report: Mass Redundancies and Career Change in Australian Journalism*. Melbourne: The New Beats Project.

# Index

For Product Safety Concerns and Information please contact our EU
representative GPSR@taylorandfrancis.com
Taylor & Francis Verlag GmbH, Kaufingerstraße 24, 80331 München, Germany